Harcourt

Reading Comprehension

Grade 5

Printed in the U.S.A.

ISBN 978-0-544-26769-5

1 2 3 4 5 6 7 8 9 10   0982   22 21 20 19 18 17 16 15 14

4500460777   A B C D E F G

Dear Parent,

Welcome to the *Core Skills Reading Comprehension* series! You have selected a unique book that focuses on developing your child's comprehension skills, the reading and thinking processes associated with the printed word. Because this series was designed by experienced reading professionals, your child will have reading success as well as gain a firm understanding of the necessary skills outlined in the Common Core State Standards.

Reading should be a fun, relaxed activity for children. They should read selections that relate to or build on their own experiences. Vocabulary should be presented in a sequential and logical progression. The selections in this series build on these philosophies to insure your child's reading success. Other important features in this series that will further aid your child include:

- Short reading selections of interest to a young reader.

- Vocabulary introduced in context and repeated often.

- Comprehension skills applied in context to make the reading more relevant.

- Multiple-choice exercises that develop skills for standardized test taking.

You may wish to have your child read the selections silently or orally, but you will find that sharing the selections and activities with your child will provide additional confidence and support to succeed. When learners experience success, learning becomes a continuous process moving them onward to higher achievements. Moreover, the more your child reads, the more proficient she or he will become.

Enjoy this special time with your child!

Sincerely,
The Educators and Staff of Houghton Mifflin Harcourt

Core Skills Reading Comprehension
GRADE 5

Table of Contents

Table of Contents
Core Skills Reading Comprehension, Grade 5

Skills Correlation

LANGUAGE ARTS SKILL	SELECTION
COMPREHENSION	
Literary Texts	
*Analyzing Visuals	4, 5, 7, 13
Cause and Effect	6, Skills Review: Selections 1–6, 7
*Characters (includes Comparing and Contrasting Characters)	3, 4, 6, 7, 12, 14
*Comparing and Contrasting Themes in Literary Works	6
Details	3, 5, 6, 7, 14
Main Ideas	3, 4, Skills Review: Selections 1–6, 7, 14
*Making Inferences	5, 7, 12, 14
*Narrator/Speaker	3, 13
Sequence of Events	3, 5, 12
*Setting (includes Comparing and Contrasting Settings)	3, 4, 5, 6
*Structure/Plot of a Literary Work	3, 5, 6, 12, ,13
*Summarizing Text	7
Theme	4, 5, 12, 14
*Using Text Evidence	6
Informational Texts	
Cause and Effect	1, Skills Review: Selections 1–6
*Comparing and Contrasting Accounts of Same Event	2
Details	1, 10, 13
Drawing Conclusions	4
Facts and Opinions	8
*Integrating Information from Different Texts	2
*Main Ideas	2, 3, Skills Review: Selections 1–6, 7, 13
*Making Inferences	1, 13
*Reasons and Evidence	2, 13
*Relationships Among Individuals, Events, or Concepts	1, 2
*Structure of Informational Text (includes Comparing and Contrasting Structure)	1, 2, 13
*Summarizing Text	2
Relevant and Irrelevant Information	3, 7, 14
Sequence	1
Text Features	3, 7

* Aligns to the Common Core State Standards for English Language Arts for grade 5

v

Skills Correlation, continued

LANGUAGE ARTS SKILL	SELECTION
VOCABULARY	
Antonyms	14
*Figurative Language	3, 4, 5, 6, 12, 13
*Idioms	3, 7
Multiple-Meaning Words	5, 12, Skills Review: Selections 12–14
Prefixes	6
Suffixes	5
Synonyms	5
Word Endings	5, Skills Review: Selections 1–6
Word Meaning	1, 3, Skills Review: Selections 1–6, 8, 10, Skills Review: Selections 7–11, 14
*Words in Context	1, 13
RESEARCH AND STUDY SKILLS	
Dictionary	4, Skills Review: Selections 1–6
Encyclopedia	4, Skills Review: Selections 1–6
Graphic Sources	5, 9, Skills Review: Selections 7–11, 13, 14, Skills Review: Selections 12–14
Outlining	9, 10, Skills Review: Selections 7–11
Parts of a Book: Table of Contents, Index, Glossary	4, Skills Review: Selections 1–6, 13, Skills Review: Selections 12–14

* Aligns to the Common Core State Standards for English Language Arts for grade 5

Selection 1: Paired

Two Brothers Who Envied Birds

From the time of the cave people and down through the ages, humans could get from one place to another only by walking. These trips were long and difficult. People saw birds flying quickly from place to place. How they envied those birds!

Then people found a way to travel faster. They rode on animals. They also had the beasts pull their vehicles. Still, the high-flying birds got to places faster. The humans were jealous.

This jealousy made people experiment with learning to fly. Why should people be stuck on the ground? After all, they were more intelligent than birds. People made wings and jumped from high places, but they never flew. They simply plummeted through the air like rocks.

In ancient times, the Greeks made up a myth about a boy named Icarus who constructed wings of feathers held together by wax. Icarus dared to fly with his wings, and he went so high that he got too close to the sun. The heat melted the wax, and poor Icarus plunged back to earth.

This myth was the Greeks' way of warning humans that their gods would punish them if they tried to soar through the air. Flying was only for insects, birds, and Greek Gods.

In the 1700s, people began to believe that, with the aid of science, they could do anything. In France, the Montgolfier brothers, Etienne and Joseph, took a turn trying to imitate the birds.

One day, as Joseph sat by his fireplace looking at the fire, he suddenly realized that the ashes floated up the chimney. Aha! He had it! Hot smoke made the ashes light enough to fly.

To experiment, Joseph filled a bag with smoke and put it in the fireplace. The bag floated up the chimney. The Montgolfier brothers did this experiment over and over with the same results each time.

In June 1783, the Montgolfiers made a big balloon of paper and a cloth called linen. They filled it with smoke from a fire. They let it go. It reached a height of 6,000 feet and landed a mile and a half away. It was a miracle! Instantly, the two brothers became famous.

At the same time, other French scientists were experimenting with hydrogen, a gas lighter than air. In August 1783, a hydrogen-filled balloon went up 3,000 feet and floated 15 miles.

The Montgolfiers continued to experiment. They soon understood that it was hot air, not smoke, that made their balloons soar. Then the King of France, Louis XVI, commanded them to send up a hot-air balloon in front of his palace located near Paris. A huge crowd came to watch on a September day in 1783.

To make the event more spectacular, the brothers had the idea of decorating the balloon and attaching a basket to it. In the basket, they placed a duck, a rooster, and a sheep, the first air passengers. The balloon took off and rose with no trouble.

The flight lasted eight minutes, but the balloon did not float very far. It came down near the palace. The waiting spectators were thrilled to discover that the passengers were fine. Someone joked that the beasts were in good physical shape, but they weren't speaking to each other.

Later, humans flew in the basket of one of the Montgolfier brothers' balloons. Now birds were not the only species to travel through the air!

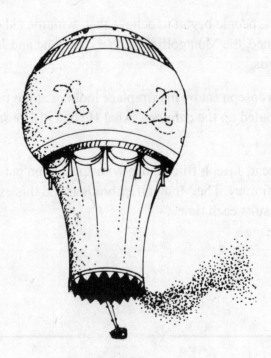

A **Circle the correct answer for each question.**

1. According to the selection, why did humans envy birds a long time ago?

   a. Birds had beautiful feathers.

   b. Birds could travel farther and faster.

   c. Birds could find homes more easily.

   d. Birds could get away from their enemies quickly.

2. What special event directly led to people's ability to make a hot-air balloon fly?

   a. Joseph Montgolfier's discovery that hot smoke made ashes rise

   b. Icarus's flight with wings made from feathers and wax

   c. King Louis XVI's command for a hot-air balloon to be sent up in the air

   d. animals being carried in a basket under a hot-air balloon

3. What is hydrogen?

   a. a type of water   c. a gas

   b. a solid   d. a metal

4. Why was hydrogen used to make hot-air balloons fly?

   a. Hydrogen is less expensive than air.

   b. Hydrogen is easier to obtain than air.

   c. Hydrogen is heavier than air.

   d. Hydrogen is lighter than air.

B **Answer the questions on the lines provided.**

1. What is the *most likely* reason that the author includes the first two paragraphs of the selection?

   _____

   _____

   _____

2. Why do you think the Montgolfier brothers put animals in the basket of the hot-air balloon?

   _____

   _____

   _____

C Write the correct word on the line to complete each sentence.

spectacular   constructed
soar   plunged
vehicle   jealous
imitate   plummet
command   myth
contracts

1. To order is to _____.

2. To envy is to be _____.

3. A truck is a heavy _____.

4. The palace was _____ of fine marble.

5. A colorful flying balloon is a _____ sight.

6. They watched the eagle _____ to the top of the cliff.

7. The diver _____ into the sea.

8. The story of Icarus is a Greek _____.

9. To act like someone else is to _____ that person.

10. To fall suddenly straight down is to _____.

D The events below tell how human beings tried to imitate birds in order to learn how to fly. The sentences are not in the correct order. Look back in the selection and then number the sentences in the right sequence. The first step is numbered for you.

_____ **a.** Joseph Montgolfier saw hot air pushing ashes up a chimney.

_____ **b.** Humans traveled in one of the Montgolfier brothers' hot-air balloons.

_____ **c.** The Montgolfiers attached a basket to a hot-air balloon and sent animals up in it.

___1___ **d.** Humans saw the swift, easy flight of birds and envied them.

_____ **e.** People made wings and jumped from high places but could not fly.

_____ **f.** The Montgolfiers filled a big balloon with smoke, and it soared into the air.

4

Selection 2: Paired

Up, Up, and Away

Joseph-Michel and Jacque-Etienne Montgolfier were born in France in the 1740s. Their father had a paper factory. The brothers were excellent observers, which helped them excel in science. They noticed how burning paper heated the air above it, so they attached a balloon to a burning pot of paper. The burning paper heated the air and made the balloon rise.

Several years passed by. Then, in September 1783, a crowd gathered near Paris, France, to witness an astounding event. The Montgolfier brothers launched the first hot-air balloon to carry passengers. Riding in a big basket attached to the balloon were three lucky riders: a duck, a sheep, and a rooster.

Even after the event had ended and the crowd had gone home, the excitement remained. Still, some people thought that humans would never fly and that Joseph-Michel and Jacque-Etienne Montgolfier were crazy.

Two months later, the brothers launched another balloon. The two men it carried became the first human passengers in a hot-air balloon. They traveled about seven miles in less than half an hour. During most of the flight, they were about 3,000 feet above the ground.

Later, hot-air balloons were improved, and they became safer. Ropes were used to keep the basket in one place until flight time. Hydrogen replaced hot air. However, it was the Montgolfier brothers who were the pioneers. They were not crazy; they had succeeded in proving that human flight could be a reality!

A Circle the correct answer for each question.

1. Which of these questions *cannot* be answered by reading the selection?

   a. How high up did the two human passengers go in the hot-air balloon?

   b. How were the two human passengers chosen to go up in the hot-air balloon?

   c. How long did the two human passengers stay up in the hot-air balloon?

   d. How far did the two human passengers travel in the hot-air balloon?

2. Which of these details belongs in a summary of the selection?

   a. The Montgolfier brothers were pioneers in the field of hot-air balloons.

   b. Some people thought the Montgolfier brothers were crazy.

   c. The first human passengers in a hot-air balloon traveled about seven miles.

   d. Two months passed between the Montgolfier brothers' first and second balloon launches.

B Think about "Up, Up, and Away" and "Two Brothers Who Envied Birds." Circle the correct answer for each question.

1. Which piece of information about the Montgolfier brothers is in **both** selections?

   a. the year in which the brothers were born

   b. the year in which scientists experimented with hydrogen

   c. the year in which a balloon filled with hydrogen was launched

   d. the year in which the brothers first launched a balloon that carried passengers

2. In each selection, read the description of the Montgolfier brothers' very first launch of a hot-air balloon. What information do you learn from "Up, Up, and Away" that is **not** found in "Two Brothers Who Envied Birds"?

   a. The event took place near Paris, France.

   b. Some people thought the brothers were crazy.

   c. The crowd watching the launch was very excited.

   d. Three animals were the passengers carried in the balloon.

3. Which of these **best** describes the organizational structure of both selections?

   a. order of importance

   b. problem and solution

   c. chronological order

   d. cause and effect

C Think about "Up, Up, and Away" and "Two Brothers Who Envied Birds." Answer the questions on the lines provided.

1. Briefly compare and contrast the brothers' first experiment described in "Up, Up, and Away" with the first experiment described in "Two Brothers Who Envied Birds."

   _____

   _____

   _____

   _____

   _____

   _____

6

2. The following conclusion could be drawn from "Up, Up, and Away" and "Two Brothers Who Envied Birds."

> It is not surprising that the Montgolfier brothers invented the hot-air balloon.

Using information from the two selections, write a paragraph that gives support for this conclusion.

_____

_____

_____

_____

_____

_____

_____

3. In which selection is it easier to tell how the author feels about the Montgolfier brothers? Support your answer with details from the selections.

_____

_____

_____

_____

_____

_____

_____

_____

7

Events in selections are often caused by something that happened before. This is called **cause** and **effect**.

cause: It is raining.   **effect:** The ground has become wet.

It is easier to work out the order in which things happen if you remember that the cause comes first and the effect follows. When putting events in order, keep that clue in mind. Often, many effects are produced by one cause.

D **Circle the letters of all the effects that could be produced by each cause given.**

1. Because people have always looked for ways to make work easier, _____
   a. they learned to use fire to cook and to heat their homes.
   b. they disliked trying new inventions.
   c. they began to use plows.
   d. they trained animals to help them work.
   e. they worked less and slept more.

2. Because people could see the sun low in the evening sky, _____
   a. they knew it would soon be night.
   b. they knew that several hours of daylight remained.
   c. they knew the sun would soon set.
   d. they knew it would soon be dawn.
   e. they knew the moon and the stars would soon be seen.

E **Choose the correct cause for each effect. Write the letter in the sentence.**

Causes

a. Because sound travels slower than light,
b. Because small streams move together and join,
c. Because the sun can affect human skin,
d. Because dinosaurs lived on Earth millions of years before humans,
e. Because the stars are very far away,
f. Because airplanes were invented,

---

1. _____ they must be studied with a telescope.

2. _____ rivers are formed.

3. _____ people can travel long distances in less time.

4. _____ no person has ever seen one.

5. _____ lightning is seen before thunder is heard.

8

Selection 3

It's funny how a word can be just that—simply a word—until you've experienced what that word expresses. From what I'm going to describe, see if you can guess which word I have in mind.

It's hard to tell who in my family is the biggest baseball fan. Mom, Dad, my sister Ellen, and I all sit glued to the TV whenever a game is on. We all listen to games on the radio if we're in a car. We all read every article about baseball in the sports magazines delivered to our house. So you can imagine our elation when Dad announced he had won tickets to the third and fourth games of the 1989 World Series. We jumped so high that we came close to touching the ceiling. (Well, maybe I'm exaggerating just a little.)

We took off early on the morning of October 17. Since our town is located only a few hours from San Francisco, we had time to be tourists before the afternoon game started. We rode the cable cars up and down the city's steep hills. We ate at a seafood restaurant at Fisherman's Wharf. We drove across the Golden Gate Bridge.

But at 5:00 sharp we were in our box seats in Candlestick Park. The Oakland A's had beaten the San Francisco Giants in the first two games. Ellen and Dad, who always cheered for the underdog, were hoping that the Giants would win. Mom and I were sticking with the A's. About 60,000 other spectators were with us in the stadium, all waiting for the "Star-Spangled Banner" to be sung followed by the first pitch.

At exactly 5:04 (I know because I was looking at my watch in anticipation), the excitement rose to new heights. But it wasn't the normal excitement around a sports event. No. Something strange was occurring at Candlestick Park. The windows in the enclosed box where our seats were started to violently shake. The tall orange light towers, which were to illuminate the playing field after nightfall, began to vibrate and then sway back and forth. Pieces of stone fell from the top stadium deck across from us. I felt the ground shift and tremble beneath my feet. But, curiously, I didn't feel afraid. It was more like a feeling of being in a movie theater—watching events from a distance rather than taking part in them.

"What's happening?" shrieked Ellen, paler than I've ever seen her because terror had drained all the color from her face. She was clinging to my mom. Then I realized that my dad's arms were tightly wrapped around me.

Some of the nearby spectators had brought radios. The voices of news announcers bleated from the radios, "Earthquake! Earthquake!"

Despite all the trembling, there was little damage to Candlestick Park. It seemed that the earthquake hadn't done too much damage. Soon the tremors stopped entirely. The players stood on the field, some of them joined by their families from the stands.

About half an hour later, we listened to the announcement that the game was canceled. Our tickets would be honored whenever and wherever the World Series was continued. Then we joined the throng exiting the stadium.

It was on our drive back to our hotel that a huge shift took place inside me. Even though I was in a car, only *looking* at the collapsed bridge and the giant cracks that ran through streets and the smashed vehicles everywhere, I started to shake uncontrollably. I felt as stunned as the people we were passing. On that slow drive back to our hotel, I had to face the horrible devastation the earthquake had caused—an earthquake I had survived without a scratch.

"Lucy, are you all right?" my mom asked me.

I could only nod. I knew that if I said something, I might start crying and not be able to stop.

We finally got back to our hotel. The building hadn't been damaged, but there was broken glass all around it. And there was no gas, electricity, or water inside. We packed our bags and started the slow drive, on streets and highways that could still be used, back to our town. Looking out the window at the crippled city, I thought about how for me—or for anyone else in San Francisco on October 17, 1989—*earthquake* would never again be just a ten-letter word on a piece of paper.

A **Circle the correct answer for each question.**

1. What does the expression "rose to new heights" (in the fifth paragraph) mean?
   a. got unexpectedly taller
   b. became greater
   c. went up in the air
   d. grew to be frightening

2. Which word in the eighth paragraph helps you understand what "tremors" means?
   a. *entirely*
   b. *players*
   c. *field*
   d. *trembling*

3. What does it mean that the "tickets would be honored" when the World Series games were continued?

   a. The spectators who survived would get medals.

   b. The spectators' tickets could be used in the future.

   c. The spectators would be given free food.

   d. The spectators would be given tickets for other baseball games.

4. What made the family decide to go to San Francisco?

   a. The father had won tickets to some baseball games.

   b. The father had won tickets to ride cable cars.

   c. The parents wanted their daughters to see what an earthquake can do.

   d. The parents wanted their daughters to see the Golden Gate Bridge.

5. Where was the family during the earthquake?

   a. in their hotel

   b. in their car

   c. in a stadium

   d. at Fisherman's Wharf

6. When did the family find out about the damage caused by the earthquake?

   a. when they first arrived in San Francisco

   b. when they rode on a cable car

   c. when they drove from the stadium to their hotel

   d. when they got to their seats at Candlestick Park

7. At the beginning of which paragraph does the narrator's tone change?

   a. third paragraph

   b. fourth paragraph

   c. ninth paragraph

   d. tenth paragraph

8. What is the *best* title for this selection?

   a. The 1989 World Series

   b. A Baseball Fan's Dream Comes True

   c. The Meaning of *Earthquake*

   d. Tourist Stops in San Francisco

B **Answer the questions on the lines provided.**

1. Compare how the narrator and her sister Ellen reacted in the stadium to the earthquake.

   _____

   _____

   _____

   _____

2. Why is the tenth paragraph important to the selection?

   _____

   _____

   _____

   _____

3. Why do you think the author wrote the selection from Lucy's point of view?

   _____

   _____

   _____

   _____

C Hit some home runs. Score by matching the correct words to the definitions. Write them next to the meanings.

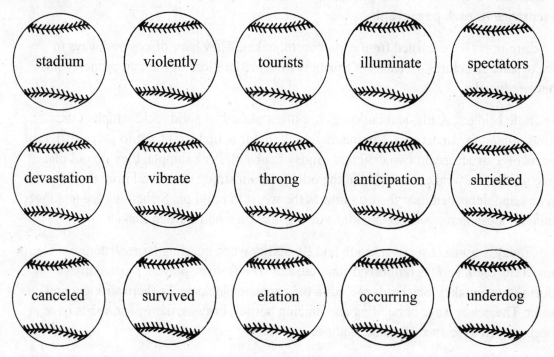

| stadium | violently | tourists | illuminate | spectators |

| devastation | vibrate | throng | anticipation | shrieked |

| canceled | survived | elation | occurring | underdog |

1. visitors who travel to see a place _____

2. to shake _____

3. lived through _____

4. to light up _____

5. a feeling of expecting something to happen _____

6. a place where sports events are held _____

7. people watching sports events _____

8. screamed or shouted _____

9. very strongly or powerfully _____

10. destruction _____

11. called off _____

12. the one not expected to win _____

13. great excitement _____

14. a large group crowded together _____

13

D Often in a paragraph, one sentence states the main idea. This sentence is called a topic sentence. It can be found anywhere in the paragraph. Read the paragraphs below. Then underline the topic sentence in each paragraph.

1. Engineers have learned from earlier earthquakes. They have discovered ways to make safer structures. Because of this new information, loss of life and property has been reduced.

2. Safe bridges, roads, and buildings are often placed on solid rock, which is the best kind of land for structures. Engineers now know it is important not to place different parts of a structure on two different kinds of subsoil. For example, they do not place one section on weaker landfill and the other part on strong rock. Soil brought down by rivers and deposited near their mouths is the worst to build on. Structures are no longer built on loose gravel and certain kinds of clay that turn liquid when shaken.

3. Today, engineers stress strength and flexibility when building large structures. The materials used, such as reinforced concrete and steel frames, prevent much damage during earthquakes. Steel rods placed in the concrete blocks make them stronger and safer. The newer ways of building and bracing houses, bridges, dams, and roads have been proved to resist earthquake damage.

4. Today, all parts of a large building must be connected so they support one another. In that way, the entire structure will vibrate evenly, preventing one part from falling and causing damage to others. In earthquakes, no one section will feel more stress than the other parts. Buildings can sway in strong winds and earth tremors but remain undamaged. Earthquake resistant buildings, in which all sections are connected, cost more, but they save money in the long run. So modern skyscrapers all over the world are built in this way.

E The details in a paragraph support the main idea. Read the following paragraphs and look at the pictures. Underline the main idea in each paragraph. On the lines after each paragraph, write the detail sentence that describes the picture.

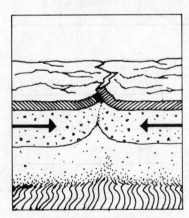

1. Pieces of the earth's crust, called **plates**, are far under the ground. They move and grind against each other. They slip over and under one another. If they meet and bump, they cause tremors in the earth. Large plates grinding violently or separating suddenly cause earthquakes.

_____

_____

14

2.   Just as in earthquakes, volcanic eruptions occur when the earth's plates bump into each other and separate. Sometimes when the plates separate, the melted, fiery rock in the center of the earth bubbles up through the crack with great force. Then all the melted rock, flame, gas, ashes, and stones erupt into the air. The melted rock, called **lava,** comes pouring out. This is a volcanic eruption.

_____

_____

3.   The Japanese word for a harbor wave is **tsunami** (tsoo nah me). **Tsunami** is now part of all languages. Earthquakes occurring anywhere set off huge waves under the ocean. These waves, called **tsunamis,** are over 100 feet high and travel 500 miles an hour. When they strike land, they destroy everything in their paths. Sometimes **tsunamis** hit near the place of the earthquake, but often they occur hundreds of miles away from the earthquake's center. Many more people are killed by the giant waves than by the earthquake tremors.

_____

_____

4.   There are steps you can take to protect yourself during an earthquake. First, try to switch off all lights to prevent electrical fires in the walls. Find a solid, strong piece of furniture such as a desk or a table and crawl under it, so falling glass or plaster will not hit you. Or you can stand in the doorway between two rooms. Doorways are braced to take stress. When the earthquake is over, go outside to a wide open space in case there are aftershocks. Stay away from downed wires.

_____

_____

15

F **Read the paragraphs below carefully. Do all the sentences give more information about the topic? If a sentence does not support the main idea of the paragraph, it is extraneous. Draw a line through every extraneous sentence.**

1.   Some people think that watching the behavior of animals can help predict an earthquake. It is said that the beasts know before humans that the earth will soon be vibrating. Some spectators claim that dogs barking without stopping signals an earthquake. Tigers, lions, leopards, pandas, and deer in China became very excited before a volcano erupted. Rats have been seen to leave their hiding places in large groups before the tremors disturbed humans. Before a forest fire, a huge army of ants carrying their eggs marched away from the woods.

2.   On the Richter Scale, numbers show how strong the tremors of earthquakes are. People do not feel the tremors unless they register 2 or above on the scale. Hurricanes are identified by the female and male names assigned to them. Some dishes are unbreakable even in earthquakes. At 5 on the Richter Scale, buildings shake. Heavy furniture turns over, chimneys fall, and walls may collapse at 6.2 on the Richter Scale. At 7, underground pipes may break. A reading of 8 on the Richter Scale can mean an area is completely destroyed. The surface of the earth is usually calm and comfortable.

3.   Do not run out into the street during an earthquake. Pieces of falling stones, bricks, and concrete may hit you as you leave the building. Tornadoes can also destroy buildings. If your home has a tile roof, stay inside because tiles are the first to fall in tremors, and their weight makes them dangerous weapons. Outdoors, do not stand close to buildings, trees, or telephone poles. The lava from a volcano can cause a great deal of damage.

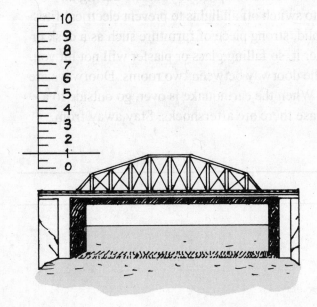
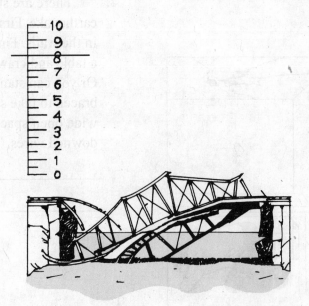

Selection 4

A Different Kind of Sand

After several days of summer storms and strong downpours, it was a relief to Brian, Kayla, and Debbie to walk on the beach again. They awoke at dawn and ran outside to watch the sun paint the sky aqua, peach, and pink as it rose in the east.

How good it felt to run on the damp sand next to the ocean! Their footprints crossed and recrossed as they jumped and jogged about. Only a few adults appeared this early on the beach. Some walked dogs. Others rode horses.

Kayla, as usual, walked toward the row of bushes growing at the far end of the beach away from the water. She had seen rabbits there last week.

Suddenly, her feet sank into the watery sand. She tried to lift them but couldn't. They seemed to be stuck as if in deep mud. "Debbie! Brian!" she shouted to her sister and brother.

The more Kayla pulled, the deeper she seemed to sink. Her legs were in the sand up to her knees. Such a thing had never happened to Kayla before.

Debbie and Brian, hearing Kayla's yells, raced towards her. "It looks as if you're in quicksand," said Brian. "I wish I could remember more about it."

"Quicksand?" echoed Kayla. "We studied that in science class, but I don't know how to get out of it. I'm afraid! It may keep pulling me down."

The children were motionless with fear, trying to decide what to do.

"Go get help! Get Mom and Dad!" Brian told Debbie.

"No!" said Kayla. "Don't leave me! I'll need both of you to pull me out."

A small group of adults had gathered. No one knew what to do. One man tried to wade to Kayla. His feet got stuck, too. But he was close enough for several people to grab him and yank him out.

Two people ran to call the police and the emergency crew. The rest watched Kayla, unable to do anything but stare.

"She's not sinking any farther," called out one woman. "That's a good sign!"

Then, a strange figure appeared. It was a boy about eleven years old who rode his horse on the beach every morning. He always dressed in a cowboy hat and boots. Kayla's family called him "the cowboy." No one ever talked to him because he kept at a distance, but everybody recognized him.

"What's going on?" the boy questioned as he cautiously approached the growing circle around Kayla.

When informed of Kayla's danger, he stared at the quicksand for a minute. Then he smiled as if there was nothing to fear.

"Don't try anything, kid," yelled a man. "Wait for the emergency crew!"

Still atop his gray and white horse, the cowboy said nothing. He grabbed the rope from his saddle, made a lasso, and swung it around.

"Everybody get ready to help pull!" he ordered.

The lasso flew out into the sand twice, missing Kayla. The cowboy moved his horse to another part of the sand so that he faced Kayla's back. Again he twirled the lasso and tossed it. This time it settled around Kayla's shoulders.

"Put it around your waist!" the cowboy directed. "Then your weight will be easier to pull."

With shaking fingers, Kayla obeyed. Then the cowboy tightened the lasso and started to pull. Everyone grabbed a part of the rope and helped tug.

For the first couple of tries, Kayla didn't move.

"You have to relax, Kayla," said Debbie. "Make yourself as limp as possible. Don't worry. We have you."

The force of the pulling knocked Kayla onto her back. Everyone froze in fear.

"It's okay," said the cowboy. "She's better off on her back because it evens out her weight on the surface. Now, everyone, grab on again and *pull*!"

This time, Kayla was pulled onto solid ground. Brian and Debbie hugged her. The crowd cheered.

Two police cars and an ambulance arrived a few minutes later. The people who had rescued Kayla were praising each other. Everyone made comments about the cowboy and his horse and how they were heroes.

The cowboy smiled, lifted his hat, and said he had to be going. Kayla said to her brother and sister, "It looks as if we'll be getting up at dawn tomorrow to find our new friend to thank him."

Name _____ Date _____

A **Circle the correct answer for each question.**

1. When did this selection take place?

   a. at sunrise   **c.** at sunset

   b. near midday   **d.** in the late afternoon

2. How did the cowboy react to a situation full of danger?

   a. with confidence, as if he knew exactly what to do

   b. with sadness, as if he were not sure that he could help

   c. with too much pride, as if he wanted to show off his skills

   d. with worry, as if he thought he might hurt Kayla while rescuing her

3. What is this selection mainly about?

   a. how quicksand is formed

   b. the rescue of someone in danger

   c. a careless girl at the beach

   d. a mysterious cowboy on a horse

4. What is the theme of the selection?

   a. Nature is full of hidden dangers.

   b. Fear makes a difficult situation even worse.

   c. Having knowledge is just as important as having skills.

   d. People working together can overcome serious problems.

5. Which of these is described in the selection using personification?

   a. the sun   **c.** the lasso

   b. the beach   **d.** the quicksand

6. How does the art in the selection *best* help you as a reader?

   a. to imagine what the cowboy's horse looks like

   b. to imagine how the cowboy is dressed when he rescues Kayla

   c. to understand how the cowboy uses his lasso

   d. to understand what the cowboy looks like on the beach every morning

© Houghton Mifflin Harcourt Publishing Company

Selection 4
Core Skills Reading Comprehension, Grade 5

After their scary adventure at the beach, Brian, Debbie, and Kayla wanted to learn more about quicksand. Debbie said, "Let's find more information about quicksand at the library."

B Use dictionary skills to answer the following questions.

1. Circle the guide words for the page that would contain *quicksand*.

   a. quote   quotient   c. quench   quiet

   b. quiver   quiz   d. quack   queen

Read this section of a dictionary page and answer the following questions.

quaint   **quill**

quaint (kwānt) *adj:* unusual or odd
quan·ti·ty (kwăn'-tĭ-tē) *n:* a number or an amount
quar·rel (kwŏr'-ĕl) **1** *n:* an angry fight **2** *v:* to find fault
quar·ry (kwŏr'-ē) *n* **1:** something that is hunted; prey **2:** place from which to get stone
queen (kwēn) *n* **1:** a female ruler; the wife of a king **2:** a playing card with the picture of a queen
ques·tion (kwĕs'-chŭn) **1** *n:* something that is asked **2** *v:* to ask
quick (kwĭk) *adj:* fast
quick·sand (kwĭk'-sănd) *n:* a loose, deep, wet sand deposit in which a heavy object or person may sink
quill (kwĭl) *n* **1:** a feather **2:** a kind of writing pen

2. How many meanings are given for the word *quarrel*?

_____

3. Which words are both a noun and a verb?

_____

4. What meaning did the dictionary give for *quicksand*? _____

_____

_____

20

5. A feather is also called a _____.

6. Which meaning of the word *quarry* is used in this sentence?

> The marble was bought from a **quarry** in New England.

_____

7. How many syllables does the word *quantity* have?

_____

8. What noun would be used for a *fox that is chased by hunters?*

_____

9. Which of these words could be used as synonyms for *quick?*

fast   quiet   rapid

speedy   quack   swift

_____

10. Which word would be used for *a person who rules over a country?*

_____

The children had learned in school where to locate information. They went to the library to get a textbook called *The Soil Under Your Feet*.

Since the whole book was about soil, they had to use the index to find their topic. This is what they knew about the index.

> 1. The *index* is at the end of a book.
> 2. It is arranged in alphabetical order.
> 3. It is used as a quick way to see if a special topic is to be found in the book.
> 4. It can also tell all the information about a special topic that can be found in the book.
> 5. It can tell on which pages the information is located.

Name _____ Date _____

C **This is part of the index of a book. Read it and answer the questions.**

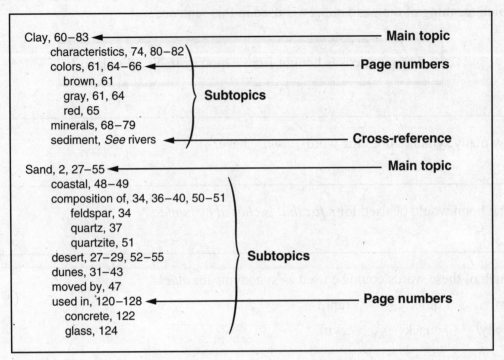

Clay, 60–83 ◄————————————————— **Main topic**
  characteristics, 74, 80–82
  colors, 61, 64–66 ◄————————————————— **Page numbers**
    brown, 61
    gray, 61, 64
    red, 65   } **Subtopics**
  minerals, 68–79
  sediment, *See* rivers ◄————————————————— **Cross-reference**

Sand, 2, 27–55 ◄————————————————— **Main topic**
  coastal, 48–49
  composition of, 34, 36–40, 50–51
    feldspar, 34
    quartz, 37
    quartzite, 51
  desert, 27–29, 52–55   } **Subtopics**
  dunes, 31–43
  moved by, 47
  used in, 120–128 ◄————————————————— **Page numbers**
    concrete, 122
    glass, 124

1. Which pages have information about desert sands?

   _____

2. On which pages can information be found on the minerals found in clay?

   _____

3. On which pages can information be found on sand dunes?

   _____

4. How many subtopics are found under *Sand?*

   _____

5. This book also tells about the topic *Loam*. Circle the place where it would be found.

   a. before *Clay*   **b.** between *Clay* and *Sand*   **c.** after *Sand*

6. Why does it say *See* rivers next to *sediment*?

   _____

Name _____ Date _____

D For further information the children turned to the encyclopedia. Look at the volumes and answer the questions.

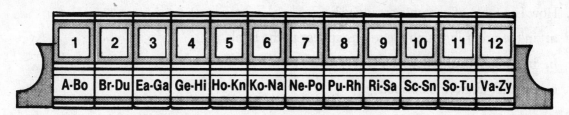

1	2	3	4	5	6	7	8	9	10	11	12
A-Bo	Br-Du	Ea-Ga	Ge-Hi	Ho-Kn	Ko-Na	Ne-Po	Pu-Rh	Ri-Sa	Sc-Sn	So-Tu	Va-Zy

1. How many volumes are in this set of encyclopedias? _____

2. In which volumes might they look for information on *desert sands*? _____ _____

3. In which volumes might they find information about *quicksand*? _____ _____

4. What beginning letters are on the three volumes in which you might find information on

   palomino and *Appaloosa horses*?   _____   _____   _____

From their search for information, the children learned these facts about *quicksand*:

1. Any sand can become quicksand. It does so when the water rises from under the sand and spreads the sand grains far apart.

2. The fine, deep, watery sand is no longer firm. It cannot support heavy weights. It is a liquid.

3. Quicksand looks the same as the nearby, ordinary solid sand.

4. When caught in quicksand, a person should not struggle. The only thing to do is to try to lie flat on one's back. A body spread out over a wider surface of sand will not sink. The person floats on the quicksand.

E Read the following sentences. Write *T* if the sentence is true, *F* if it is false, and *N* if not enough information was given.

_____ 1. Quicksand is dry soil that pulls small objects down.

_____ 2. Quicksand is fine, deep, liquid sand.

_____ 3. When a person is lying flat, his or her body can float on the quicksand.

_____ 4. Another name for *quicksand* is *livesand*.

_____ 5. The bones of dinosaurs are found in quicksand.

_____ 6. Pulling and pushing one's feet in the quicksand helps a person get out.

_____ 7. When caught in quicksand, the best thing to do is to lie flat.

_____ 8. Quicksand is solid.

Circle the correct answer for each question. If you need to see a table of contents, look at the one in this book.

1. How is a table of contents arranged?

   a. in the order in which the topics appear in the book

   b. in alphabetical order

   c. Neither answer is correct.

2. How is an index arranged?

   a. chapter by chapter

   b. in alphabetical order

   c. Neither answer is correct.

3. Which one would be arranged like this?

Chapter I—Origin of the Horse	3
Chapter II—Kinds of Horses	28
Chapter III—Diseases of Horses	47

   a. the table of contents

   b. the index

   c. neither of them

4. Which one is a list of words, their meanings, and their pronunciations?

   a. the table of contents

   b. the index

   c. neither of them

5. Which one divides the words into syllables?

   a. index

   b. dictionary

   c. table of contents

6. Which one is arranged in alphabetical order?

   a. table of contents

   b. encyclopedia

   c. neither of them

24

Selection 5: Paired

To Gain Something Lost

The clop of horses' hooves and the shouts of people rang through the forest. Hidden in a woodcutter's hut, the twins giggled. Enid and Edward had caused all this excitement!

A group of soldiers dismounted to more closely inspect the ground. One of them said, "I think it went up the hill."

"Sire," another soldier called out. "Hoofprints. The unicorn came in this direction."

Lord John, Lady Isabel, and the men with them prepared to follow the tracks. How eager they were to find that never-before-captured beast, the unicorn!

In their hiding place, the twins could barely control their laughter. They knew that the hoofprints had not been made by the magic feet of the imaginary animal.

Lord John ordered, "We will go around the hill to head it off before it reaches the fields."

Suddenly Lady Isabel cried, "Wait. We are wasting our time. These cannot be the hoofprints of a unicorn."

"What do you mean, my Lady?" asked the steward, who took care of the castle.

"Look. The beast that made these prints is wearing iron horseshoes," explained Lady Isabel. "A unicorn would not be wearing horseshoes. And—equally as important—the horseshoes it is wearing are just like those made by our blacksmith!"

25

"Fooled again!" exclaimed Lord John. "It is the work of the blacksmith's wicked children once more!"

"Another one of their tricks. They should be punished," the steward said gravely.

Suddenly, the twins stopped smiling. This time, their prank had been discovered before they had fled from the scene.

It took less than a minute for the soldiers to find Enid and Edward in the hut. A gray horse with a wooden horn tied to its head nibbled the grass nearby.

"And that unicorn is really *my* gray mare!" shrieked Lady Isabel. "Oh, you wicked, wicked children! You made all these soldiers leave the castle unprotected to chase after a fake unicorn!"

In those days—the year was 1280—the lord who owned the land ruled over everyone who lived there. Enid, Edward, and their parents were dragged into the Great Hall of Lord John's castle to hear their punishment.

"If you were not the best blacksmith in the region," thundered the steward to the twins' father, "I would order all of you to leave this land forever."

"How old are you, children?" asked Lord John.

Enid and Edward bowed. "Nine years old, Sire," they said together.

"Why are you not working from sunrise to sunset like everyone else?" asked Lady Isabel.

"Forgive them, my Lady," begged the blacksmith. "They are quick, good workers. Edward is so fast in my forge that we often finish making all the needed tools and horseshoes well ahead of time. He will someday be the best blacksmith in all of England."

"What about the young girl?" asked Lord John.

"Enid is just the same," explained their mother. "She spins thread faster than any woman in the village. Then she plays pranks when her work is finished."

The steward said to Lord John, "It is true, Sire. They are among the best workers in your service. But I also have a list of their wrongdoings. Let me tell you what is perhaps their most serious one. Last year, they spread a story that a fire-eating dragon lived in the lake. They faked the smoke that supposedly floated from the dragon's nostrils. Not a seed was planted near the lake for two weeks because, of course, the villagers were too frightened of the dragon. This affected the harvest later. Also, the villagers left their sheep unguarded, and one of them was killed by a wolf."

26

Enid realized that now was the time to speak up. "Please, Sire," she said to Lord John. "We made the horse look like a unicorn because the one you have on your shield and on the castle banner is so beautiful."

Edward followed his sister's lead. "We only wanted to make you and Lady Isabel happy. We wanted you to think there was a real unicorn on your land like the one on your flag and shield."

"You have been so good to us," continued Enid, "that we wanted to do something for you in return."

The Lord's and Lady's anger melted. They both smiled at the twins.

The blacksmith looked at his children and whispered to them, "Now no one will ever believe you two. Any time you need help in the future, people will think it is another of your tricks."

For punishment, the steward commanded the twins to work outside the castle walls gathering firewood whenever they finished their regular work. Thus, it happened that one night they returned late to the castle. They moaned when they saw that the drawbridge was raised. "Now we cannot get across the moat," Edward said, pointing to the large ditch that surrounded the castle.

In those days, poor children were used to sleeping outdoors from time to time. Enid and Edward lay down in the darkness. They hoped that soon someone important would need to enter or leave the castle, causing the guards to lower the drawbridge.

27

The twins were almost asleep when they heard a strange sound. Peering through the darkness, they saw a small boat in the moat near the back square towers of the castle. The guards high in the towers did not see or hear what was happening. The twins watched in silence for what seemed like hours. Men in the boat appeared to be working with something at the base of the right tower.

When Edward and Enid told their father the next morning about what they had seen, he laughed. When they told the captain of the guards, he growled, "Ha! Another one of your jokes. You cannot fool me this time."

For the next ten nights, the twins stayed outside the castle to watch the strangers. It seemed as if the men in the boat were loosening a stone on the corner of the tower just above the water.

Like all poor people in England at that time, the twins and their parents depended on Lord John's soldiers for protection. They, in turn, helped the castle owner fight off enemies when there was danger. If the castle were captured, all the inhabitants would be killed. So everyone had to work together. Edward and Enid guessed that the men in the boat were enemy soldiers. Nobody, however, would listen to the children.

The next day, Edward and Enid checked the inside of the tower to see what the strangers had done. They crept into one of the dark cellars and felt their way through a passage into the bottom of the tower. What a shock it was to discover that thirty large stones were loose and ready to be pushed out!

"They can bring in an entire army late at night in boats," Edward said fearfully. "They will creep in through this hole and take our soldiers by surprise."

The twins tried to warn Lady Isabel of the danger. She replied, "I cannot believe a word you say."

"Someone inside the castle may be helping the enemy," Enid told Edward. "Let's watch from inside. If we find out who it is, someone may believe us."

That night they tiptoed through the cellars armed with two pieces of iron from their father's forge. This time, they could hear the sound of the enemies' tools picking at the stones. A dark shadow stood inside the tower speaking to the strangers. "Tomorrow night the opening will be large enough for the attack." The twins froze. They recognized that voice! "Have all the boatloads of soldiers here by two hours past midnight. We will surprise Lord John while he sleeps. Then I will be the ruler of the castle and of this land!"

Enid and Edward were amazed. It was the steward! He was helping the enemy. In fact, he was the enemy! In his surprise, Edward cried out.

The steward whirled around. Sword in hand, he rushed at the children and yelled in rage. They stepped back and raised their iron bars to protect themselves. It was an uneven fight. The blacksmith's children were quick and small. The steward was large, and the passage was too narrow for him to raise his huge sword. Enid and Edward knocked him down.

All the noise and shouting brought the guards down into the cellars. They seized the steward and his helpers. One of the guards went to inform Lord John that the castle had nearly been attacked. Lord John dashed to the scene and saw that his trusted steward had betrayed him.

From now on, neither he, nor any other adult, would think that the twins were playing a trick on them.

Realizing they had saved the lives of everyone in the castle made the twins very happy. They had also learned an important lesson about trust.

A **Circle the correct answer for each question.**

1. What did Lord John and Lady Isabel believe they were hunting?

   a. a lost horse

   b. children who were lost

   c. animals to kill for food

   d. a rare unicorn

2. Why did adults not trust the twins?

   a. They were often careless.

   b. They had played too many tricks.

   c. They helped Lord John's enemies.

   d. They cheated and stole from people.

3. How did the enemy plan to capture the castle?

   a. by bringing troops by boat to climb the outside of the tower

   b. by digging a tunnel under the castle and entering the Great Hall

   c. by breaking down the drawbridge over the moat

   d. by entering through a hole made in the bottom of a tower

4. Which of these events happened last?

   a. The twins pretended to have seen a fire-breathing dragon.

   b. The twins slept on the ground outside the castle walls.

   c. The steward rushed toward the twins with his sword.

   d. No one believed the twins' story about the loose stones.

29

5. Why is is the steward's description of the fire-eating dragon, the harvest, and the flock of sheep important to the selection?

   a. It helps you understand that not all of the twins' tricks were about unicorns.

   b. It helps you understand that the twins' tricks were sometimes harmful.

   c. It helps you understand how evil the steward could be.

   d. It helps you understand how dangerous life was in the year 1280.

6. Which of these is the *best* clue to the setting of the selection?

   a. The twins liked to play tricks on people.

   b. The twins tried to warn adults of danger.

   c. The twins hid in a woodcutter's hut.

   d. The twins were quick, good workers.

7. In which part of the selection does the excitement build to its highest point?

   a. the part in which the twins protect themselves from the steward in the narrow passage

   b. the part in which Lord John sees for himself that the steward has betrayed him

   c. the part in which the steward says that his soldiers will attack the castle the next morning

   d. the part in which the twins discover that stones are ready to be pushed out by enemy soldiers

8. The author says that Lord John's and Lady Isabel's "anger melted." What do these words show?

   a. Their blood was boiling from realizing they had been tricked.

   b. Their anger was so great that it made them feel hot.

   c. They thought the twins were telling the truth.

   d. They were no longer mad at the twins.

9. Read the title of the selection. What was lost and gained?

   a. happiness

   b. friendship

   c. trust

   d. loyalty

B **Answer the questions on the lines provided.**

1. The twins said that they made the fake unicorn because they wanted Lady Isabel and Lord John to be happy by thinking there was a real unicorn on their land like the one on their shield and banner. How do you know the twins were not telling the truth when they said this?

_____

_____

_____

_____

2. Name two ways that the illustration on page 25 helps you understand the selection.

_____

_____

_____

_____

31

C **Read each sentence below. Write the correct word form to complete each sentence.**

suggest suggests suggested suggesting suggestion

1. Lord John would not accept the steward's _____ to keep the drawbridge down all day long.

2. A year before, Lady Isabel had _____ that more guards be stationed on the walls.

3. While Mother was _____ that Enid should spin more carefully, she was interrupted.

4. Edward was able to _____ some faster ways to heat the iron.

5. Lord John is only _____ that you go hunting. You must decide.

D **Climb the tower. Match each word with its synonym. Write the synonym beside the word.**

1. commanded _____

2. imaginary _____

3. inspect _____

4. fled _____

5. moat _____

6. nibbled _____

7. captured _____

8. banner _____

9. scene _____

10. pranks _____

a. examine

b. tricks

c. make-believe

d. location

e. ordered

f. escaped

g. caught

h. surprise

i. ate

j. ditch

k. flag

E **Read the selection below. Use the words in dark type to label the parts of the drawing.**

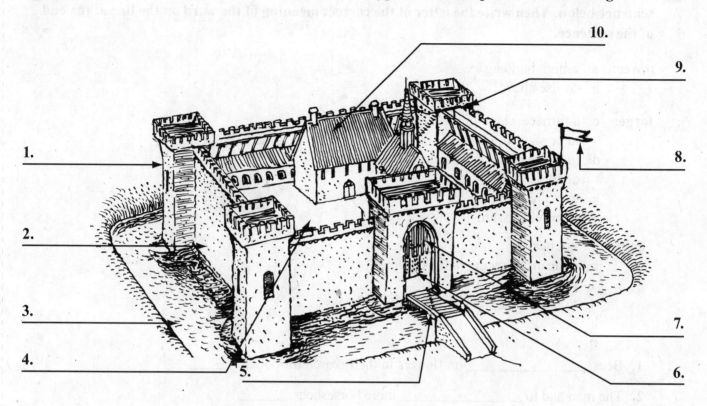

Lord John and Lady Isabel Bracey were invited to the king's castle. With their steward and soldiers, this is how they entered the well-protected building.

As the party approached the castle, they first saw the four square **towers**. Between the towers stretched a thick, strong stone **wall**. Along the wall and the tops of the towers were **battlements**. The king's soldiers could fire arrows at enemies and then hide behind the battlements for safety.

From the highest tower flew the special **banner** of the king. The guards in the towers checked to see if the Lord John was an enemy. Then they lowered the **drawbridge** so the visitors could cross the deep **moat**.

At the end of the drawbridge, the visitors faced a heavy iron gate. It was called the **portcullis**. Guards raised it by turning a large wheel. Behind the gate was a heavy wooden **door**. Guards raised a huge bar to open it.

Lord John and his group then entered a **courtyard**. Again, guards inspected them by looking through tiny arrow slits in the walls. Finally, the group was led inside the castle to the **Great Hall**.

33

F Look at the different meanings of *tower*, *forge*, and *light*. Write the correct word in each sentence below. Then write the letter of the correct meaning of the word on the line at the end of the sentence.

tower: a. a high building
        b. to rise above

forge: c. a furnace where iron is heated
           to be shaped
        d. to shape metal as a blacksmith
           does
        e. to make a fake object
        f. to move forward

light: g. not heavy
        h. a means of seeing in the darkness
        i. to land on something
        j. to make it possible to see in the darkness
        k. pale

1. Bees _____ on flowers in their search for pollen. _____

2. The man had to _____ more horseshoes. _____

3. Start the fire in the _____ . _____

4. Use this torch to _____ the way through the tunnel. _____

5. The large package is _____ enough to carry easily. _____

6. She wore a _____ gray coat. _____

7. See how the oak trees _____ over the bushes. _____

8. The soldiers began to _____ ahead. _____

G Suffixes are endings added to root words to change the meaning. Adding the suffix *-ion* to some verbs changes them into nouns. Circle the correct word to complete each sentence. Look carefully at each root word.

Examples:

    Lady Isabel made an *inspection* of the hoofprints. Edward made a *suggestion* about
    how to capture the enemies.

1. The pipe _____ was loose.

    connection   convention   collection

2. His _____ made us laugh at him.

    locations   inspections   actions

34

3. A light will help you discover the _____ of the loose stones.

    election   connection   location

4. They asked everyone to attend the event by sending _____.

    actions   invitations   conditions

5. After Lord John's _____ of the tower, the servant was ordered to clean it.

    inspection   instruction   invitation

6. The new _____ was stopped after high winds knocked down the walls.

    location   construction   information

7. The soldiers marched in the _____ of the river.

    election   direction   inspection

8. To learn how to shoot with a bow and arrow, you must follow my _____.

    directions   elections   inspections

H Study the map below. Then answer the following questions. Write the letter next to the question.

KEY   🐴 Stable   ∩ Blacksmith's Forge   ▣ Tower

           🌀 Well   ▭▭▭ Thick Wall   🌀 Spiral Stairs

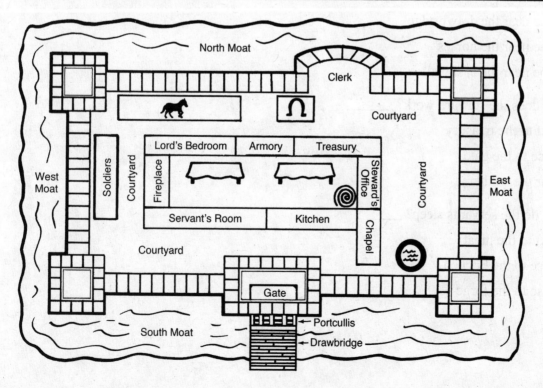

© Houghton Mifflin Harcourt Publishing Company

1. Where is the forge? _____
   a. next to the stable
   b. next to the kitchen
   c. by the main gate

2. Where are the living quarters for the soldiers? _____
   a. next to the well
   b. near the east wall
   c. near the west wall

3. Where is the drawbridge? _____
   a. next to the fireplace
   b. the north end of the Great Hall
   c. close to the gate

4. How many towers are there? _____
   a. four   b. two   c. three

5. Where is the well? _____
   a. by the spiral stairs
   b. at the south end of the courtyard
   c. next to the stable

6. Why is the blacksmith located by the stable? _____
   a. to be near the drawbridge
   b. to be near the horses
   c. to be near the east wall

7. Where does the steward work? _____
   a. next to the treasury
   b. close to the gate
   c. near the soldiers

8. Where do the servants sleep? _____
   a. next to the moat
   b. close to the kitchen
   c. close to the forge

Selection 6: Paired

The Boy Who Cried Wolf

A ten-year-old boy may be unable to cut down trees or clear fields or build a house. But he certainly can watch over sheep and shout a warning if danger approaches. That is why boys have been shepherds in many places and at many times throughout history.

Walter was one such shepherd. Every morning he took his family's flock of sheep down a steep hill. Thick grass grew in the valley at the bottom. Every day until sundown, Walter watched over the sheep, always with great care. Well, almost always . . .

It is impossible for a ten-year-old shepherd not to get bored every once in a while, especially in a place where seeing other people was unusual. So to amuse himself, Walter sometimes did things that distracted him from doing his duty. On some days, he would leave the sheep unprotected as he tracked a deer's prints or chased after a rabbit. On other days, he would run among the sheep, making them scatter in different directions. Then he would have fun reordering them into a proper flock.

Each day passed by slowly for Walter. But one day in particular seemed to drag on as if it never wanted to reach its end. On that day, maybe because he was feeling more impatient than usual, an idea hatched in Walter's head. If his idea worked, he would amuse himself and have company in this lonely place.

He smiled and cried, "Help! Help! A wolf is nearby!"

His plan worked. Hiding the smile as best he could, he watched a large group of villagers run down the hill toward him.

"Where is the wolf?" cried the baker.

Walter exploded in laughter. "Your faces as you ran down the hill . . . they were the funniest thing I've seen in a long time!"

The villagers grumbled in anger.

"We left our work to come help you—," said the teacher.

"And we ran all the way—," said the gray-haired tailor.

"Only to find that you were misbehaving," said the blacksmith.

"I was just having a little fun," Walter told them. But they were already trudging back up the hill.

A week passed by, each day more boring than the one before it. Walter knew he shouldn't repeat the same prank, but he did anyway.

"Help! Help!" he cried. "Three wolves are circling my flock!"

Once again a group of villagers—though much smaller this time—ran down the hill. Right away they realized that the shepherd, bent over with laughter, had tricked them again. As they started up the hill, the village mayor stayed behind long enough to say, "Walter, if you don't change your ways, misfortune will surely find you."

"Not me!" said Walter with a grin.

But the mayor's prediction proved to be true. A few days later Walter, feeling bored, was stirring up an anthill with a stick. As he observed the ants scurrying around, his entire flock started bleating. He looked up and saw a wolf a short distance away, observing his sheep!

Walter knew the animal was looking for the young, old, or hurt among his flock. "Help! Help!" he cried. "A wolf is about to attack my sheep!"

Not one villager came down the hill.

"Help!" he cried again. "This time there really is a wolf!"

Still no one came.

Walter knew he couldn't kill the wolf by himself. So he dashed to the village and shouted for help.

"Silly boy. After all your tricks, we'll never be able to trust you," said the baker.

The frantic bleating of Walter's sheep floated up the hill and into his ears. He sat down on a bench and cried long and hard for himself and his flock.

38

A Circle the correct answer for each question.

1. Who tried to help Walter by giving him advice?

   a. the baker

   c. the teacher

   b. the mayor

   d. the blacksmith

2. The events in the selection happen because

   a. Walter could not cut down trees.

   c. Walter chased a rabbit.

   b. Walter made his sheep scatter.

   d. Walter was bored.

3. Why is the third paragraph important to the selection?

   a. It helps the reader understand why Walter would play a trick on the villagers.

   b. It helps the reader understand the author's purpose for writing the selection.

   c. It helps the reader imagine the life of a shepherd.

   d. It helps the reader feel sorry for Walter's sheep.

4. The author used personification to describe

   a. misfortune.

   c. the valley.

   b. the wolf.

   d. impatience.

5. Which of these sentences *best* supports the theme of the selection?

   a. *Walter knew he shouldn't repeat the same prank, but he did anyway.*

   b. *"I was just having a little fun," Walter told them.*

   c. *"Silly boy. After all your tricks, we'll never be able to trust you," said the baker.*

   d. *The frantic bleating of Walter's sheep floated up the hill and into his ears.*

6. Which of these things about the setting is *most* important to the plot?

   a. Thick grass grows in the valley.

   c. Few people are ever in the valley.

   b. The valley is at the bottom of a steep hill.

   d. Deer and rabbits live in the valley.

B Answer the question on the lines provided.

Walter pretended that a wolf was threatening his flock of sheep. Contrast what he thought about this trick with what the villagers thought about it.

_____

_____

_____

_____

Name _____ Date _____

C **Think about "To Gain Something Lost" and "The Boy Who Cried Wolf." Then answer the
questions on the lines provided.**

1. Who is the narrator in "To Gain Something Lost"? _____

   Who is the narrator in "The Boy Who Cried Wolf"? _____

2. What trick do Enid and Edward play in "To Gain Something Lost"? _____

   _____

   What trick does Walter play in "The Boy Who Cried Wolf"? _____

   _____

3. What lesson do Enid and Edward learn in "To Gain Something Lost"? _____

   _____

   What lesson does Walter learn in "The Boy Who Cried Wolf"? _____

   _____

4. Is the ending of "To Gain Something Lost" happy or sad? _____

   Is the ending of "The Boy Who Cried Wolf" happy or sad? _____

5. Using your answers for questions 1–4, write a paragraph in which you compare and contrast
   "To Gain Something Lost" and "The Boy Who Cried Wolf."

   _____

   _____

   _____

   _____

   _____

   _____

   _____

   _____

Selection 6: Paired
Core Skills Reading Comprehension, Grade 5

D A prefix is a word part added to a root word to change the meaning. The chart tells you the meaning of a few prefixes. In each pair of words below the chart, only one of the words is a root word with a prefix. Circle this word in each pair.

Prefix	Meaning
im-	not
re-	again
mis-	not

1. missed
   mistrust

2. impatient
   imagine

3. restate
   reach

4. important
   imperfect

5. under
   unusual

6. recess
   reorder

7. misunderstand
   miserable

8. unexpected
   uncle

9. misbehave
   mist

E Read each sentence below. Choose the correct word to complete each sentence.

| unprotected | resend | impolite | unable | reset | impatient |

1. Since you never received my e-mail, I will _____ it.

2. Some of the students were _____ to finish the test in one hour.

3. The _____ child ate dinner with her fingers.

4. The storm made the electricity go out, and Mom had to _____ the clock after it came back on.

5. When the dog ran away, the sheep were left _____.

41

Skills Review: Selections 1–6

A Choose the correct word to complete each sentence. Some words may be used more than once.

> **direct**   **directly**   **directed**   **directing**   **direction**

1. A balloon can move only in the _____ the wind takes it.

2. There was no one _____ traffic after the accident.

3. When they felt the tremor, the police officer _____ them to a safe place.

4. The village was _____ in the way of the lava.

5. When the bridge collapsed, firefighters had to _____ vehicles to other streets.

6. People had to find ways to steer a hot-air balloon in a certain _____.

> **occur**   **occurs**   **occurred**   **occurring**   **occurrence**

7. Scientists still cannot predict when an earthquake will _____.

8. The _____ of an earthquake stopped the World Series.

9. A tsunami wave sometimes _____ after earthquakes.

10. An earthquake is a terrible _____.

11. It _____ to the cowboy that he could lasso Kayla.

12. Walter was responsible for what had _____.

13. Enid and Edward knew what was _____ in the castle.

B Choose words from the box to complete the crossword puzzle.

amaze	excite	shepherd	on
bridge	fled	scene	go
capture	forge	steward	ill
cellars	inspect	moat	we
dismount	towers	unicorn	net
dragon	dashed	one	

ACROSS

1. to get off a horse
5. to look carefully at
7. to leave
9. to catch
10. opposite of *off*
11. to cause strong feeling
13. a fish catcher
15. got away fast
17. you and I
18. to surprise
19. something to help you cross deep water
20. location
21. someone who watches over sheep

DOWN

1. imaginary fire-breathing beast
2. ditch filled with water
3. animal never captured by humans
4. furnace for melting iron
6. one who takes care of a castle
8. a number
9. basements
12. sick
14. tall, narrow buildings
16. ran fast

43

C The topic sentence of a paragraph is not always the first sentence. It can be found anywhere in a paragraph. Read the following paragraphs. Underline the topic sentence in each.

1. A saddle is a seat used by a person riding on a horse. The saddle is placed on the animal's back. A strap from the saddle fastens under the horse's body. It keeps the saddle from slipping off. The stirrups hang down from it. The rider's feet go in the stirrups. Most saddles are made of leather.

2. We left home early, but the car wouldn't start. While we were walking to the bus, a dog ran by and grabbed my notebook. We stopped in a restaurant to alert the police about the runaway dog. We had pancakes and orange juice while we waited. Finally, the police came and asked us a million questions. A police car was bringing me to school, but we had to stop to fix a flat tire. That's why I'm two hours late for school, Mr. Patel.

3. The trees in the neighborhood were bright with color. Red, yellow, orange, and brown replaced the green of summer. Slowly the days became shorter. Autumn was bringing its many changes. At last, the trees were becoming bare. At the same time, the weather was getting colder.

4. Sometimes, sailors landed on islands in the Pacific Ocean to get fresh water and food. One of their favorite foods was the fresh meat of the large turtles. They killed, cooked, and ate them on the islands. When they went back to their ships, they took live turtles with them so they would always have fresh meat. They would kill a turtle anytime the cook wanted to prepare a fresh meat dish.

D Sometimes the main idea of a paragraph is understood but not stated. Under the following paragraph, write the main idea. It is not directly stated in the paragraph, but it can be clearly understood.

  Matilda and Thomas had to awaken early to do their chores. They fed the chickens first. Then they collected the eggs. Cleaning their room was the next task. Then they went out to the well to bring in pails of water. Father had already started a fire in the fireplace. Last of all, the children cleaned the oil lamps and refilled them. The whole family was proud of those lamps, so Matilda and Thomas were very careful. Grandma had their lunch buckets ready. Mother gave them each bread and cornmeal mush, which they ate in a hurry. Then they rushed off to school.

_____

_____

_____

Name _____ Date _____

E Label each example and answer each question using the following terms: *index, table of contents, dictionary, encyclopedia,* or *map.*

---

ocrea	odic

oc·ta·gon (ôk-tâ-gun) *n:* polygon having eight sides

oc·tag·o·nal (ôk-tâg-ô-nəl) *adj:* having eight angles
    and eight sides

---

1. _____

Sports, 215–219, 227–233, 307, 340–348;
    bicycling, 230, 342;
    fishing, 340, 346–348;
    hiking, 228–231, 345;
    karate, 340–342;
    skating, 347;
    swimming, 342–344, 348

2. _____   3. _____

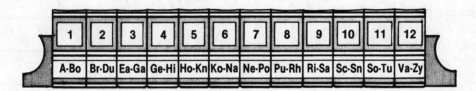

1	2	3	4	5	6	7	8	9	10	11	12
A-Bo	Br-Du	Ea-Ga	Ge-Hi	Ho-Kn	Ko-Na	Ne-Po	Pu-Rh	Ri-Sa	Sc-Sn	So-Tu	Va-Zy

4. _____

5. _____

6. In which of these would you look to see how many pages a certain book has about the Arabian Sea?

_____   _____

7. In which of these would you look to learn how to pronounce *alopecia*?

_____

8. In which of these would you look to find the closest large city to the small town of Middletown,

New York? _____

Skills Review: Selections 1–6
Core Skills Reading Comprehension, Grade 5

F Here is part of the index from a book. See if you remember how to locate information in an index. Answer the following questions.

Motion pictures, 4, 15–50	instruments, 70, 81–129
acting schools, 16, 19	cymbals, 71–75
cartoons, 24–33	drums, 70, 76–79, 92–96
Disney, Walt, 28–30	guitar, 81–85, 114, 116–118
Hollywood, 20, 34, 42, *photo* 35	piano, 118, 127–129
museums, 17, 18, 21–23	Japanese, 150, 153, 154
costumes, 45	Television, 6, 200–252
locations, 43	advertising, 202, 230–239
stage sets, 46–50	cameras, 220–227
Music, 3, 65–154	educational, 210, 218
African, 65–75, 91	electronic games, 241–248, 250–252
American, 100, 112–117	taping, 239, 249–251
Chinese, 96–98	use of satellites, 200, 201
Indian, 142, 145, 147–149	

1. On what pages could you look to find out if Walt Disney is still living? _____

2. How many subtopics are given for television? _____

3. Would this book give you any information about a trumpet? _____

4. What page would help you see what Hollywood looks like? _____

5. How many pages could you check to find out how satellites help you see

   television programs? _____

6. Is there any information in this book that tells you how to buy a television set? _____

7. Which would be the best page to start to read about Indian music? _____

8. Are there more pages on Chinese music than on Japanese music? _____

9. Under the subtopic *instruments*, which ones are discussed?

   _____

10. If the author had included Greek music in the book, where would this subtopic appear?

   _____

G **Choose the correct effect for each cause. Circle it.**

1. Because Dad won the tickets,

    a. the family went to West Virginia.

    b. his name was announced at the game.

    c. the family went to California.

2. Because there was no electricity,

    a. people used flashlights and candles.

    b. automobiles could not start.

    c. batteries did not work.

3. Because the family lived close to San Francisco,

    a. they took a taxi.

    b. they flew with the baseball team.

    c. they traveled by car.

4. Because the earthquake occurred,

    a. the game started early.

    b. some games were canceled.

    c. no tickets were honored.

H **Choose the correct cause for each effect. Write the letter in the sentence.**

Causes

a. Because Icarus flew too near the sun

b. Because scientists wanted to know how strong earthquakes were

c. Because birds fly fast and easily

d. Because huge plates under the earth collided

e. Because the family traveled to San Francisco

f. Because hydrogen is lighter than air

---

1. _____, they made the Richter Scale.

2. _____, people wanted to imitate them.

3. _____, the wax on his feathers melted.

4. _____, the light towers swayed and trembled.

5. _____, the balloons soared into the sky.

Selection 7

My name is Donna Chang. I don't mean to brag, but I'm a detective. You can be a detective, too. Just watch carefully, listen when people talk to you, and think.

This case started last Monday. Mrs. Jordan kept my friend Liz after school. I stood just outside the door to wait for her. Mrs. Jordan told Liz that a new girl would be entering our class the next day. Our teacher wanted Liz to show the new student around. She asked Liz to make the new student feel at home in a strange place.

On our way to school Tuesday morning, Liz said, "I'll tell you a secret. Mrs. Jordan has a special reason this time for asking me to help the new girl. Her name is Joanne Smart."

"Don't say another word!" I interrupted. "Anyone with the last name of Smart is going to get a lot of teasing about it! Mrs. Jordan wants you to stop the kids from making fun of the new girl."

"There's Donna acting like a detective again!" exclaimed Glenn, Liz's older brother.

Liz nodded her head. "You're right, Donna," she said. "I'm supposed to make sure that no one hurts Joanne's feelings."

My brother Nicky started to giggle as we got to the school playground. "It'll be easy to find Joanne! She'll be the one with the big brain!"

Glenn, Liz, and I scolded Nicky until he promised to be quiet. Then I gazed around the school grounds, trying to find which one in the mob of noisy students was Joanne.

I looked and thought, "If I were new, where would I stay until the bell rang? The door! I'd hang around the door sizing up the kids."

We moved closer to the door. I spotted a girl.

"There she is!" I said. "I'll bet that's Joanne."

"Oh, come on!" moaned Glenn. "The great detective strikes again. How do you know that's Joanne?"

I explained, "She's got an adult with her. It's probably her father bringing her for the first day. She's got that I-dare-you-to-make-fun-of-my-name look in her eyes. She's nervous, but she's not afraid. Because her name is Smart, she's learned to protect herself."

"Hey, Donna!" said Glenn. "I dare you to tell us more about that girl. A smart detective like you should be able to give us her whole biography!"

Whenever people say things like that to me, I'm ready to go on the warpath. They could be detectives, too. All they have to do is listen carefully, watch, and think.

I watched the girl for a while longer. Then I saw some things. I thought about them.

"Okay. Here's what I think," I said. "That girl, whoever she is, does a lot of writing. She probably always has her homework done. She writes with her left hand. Just a short time ago, she probably had a broken leg. She's outdoors often when it's dark. It might be that she delivers newspapers."

"Wow!" said Nicky. "You're really out on a limb now! How can you know all that?"

"I'm sure of some of it," I answered.

"We'll find out in class," said Liz just as the bell rang.

I was right about one thing. The girl we had been watching *was* in our class. Mrs. Jordan introduced her to Liz as Joanne. Liz showed Joanne the lockers, the cafeteria, and the library. She introduced her to the other students.

By lunchtime, I thought Joanne felt comfortable enough to answer a few questions.

Liz told her what I had said.

Joanne's eyes grew wide. "How did you know? It's all true!"

"Anyone can tell," I said, and then I explained how.

"People who write a lot get a bump on the middle finger bone where they hold a pencil. Joanne's bump is on her left hand."

"Now look at her blue and yellow tennis shoes," I said. "The right one looks like new. The left one is faded and worn. How can that be? The right one hasn't been worn much. Joanne could only have walked about with one shoe if she had a walking cast on the other foot. That could mean her right leg was broken. Now that it's healed, Joanne is wearing both shoes." The other students nodded in agreement.

I went on. "See the stripes on Joanne's jacket. They're the kind that shine in the dark. That means she's out walking, running, or riding her bike at night. There's a black spot on the jacket. It looks like newsprint, which comes off on everything. It could come from newspapers that Joanne delivers. Putting the spot and the stripes together might mean that Joanne is out in the dark delivering morning papers."

"You're like a detective, Donna!" Joanne exclaimed.

I smiled. Then I looked at my friends with an I-told-you-so look. They looked back at me with amazement.

Everyone got so excited about Joanne that they forgot to ask her last name. By the time they found out, she was too well-liked and respected for much teasing. Joanne often thanked me for helping her get accepted so quickly by her new classmates.

A Circle the correct answer to each question.

1. Why was Mrs. Jordan worried about Joanne?
   a. She thought the other students would make fun of Joanne.
   b. She thought the other students would ignore Joanne.
   c. She thought Joanne would be too shy to speak to the other students.
   d. She thought Joanne would have trouble walking around the school.

2. Which of these did Liz *not* do for Joanne the first day?
   a. Liz taught Joanne to find her way around the school.
   b. Liz helped Joanne to feel at home in a new school.
   c. Liz told the other students to be nice to Joanne.
   d. Liz introduced Joanne to some of the students.

3. How do you think Joanne felt as she stood by the school door?
   a. proud and happy
   b. calm and pleased with herself
   c. jealous and angry
   d. frightened and excited

4. Why was Donna sure that Joanne had had a broken leg?
   a. She was walking with crutches.
   b. There was a cast on her leg.
   c. She limped when she walked.
   d. One shoe looked worn, but the other looked new.

5. Why did Joanne *not* need much protection?
   a. She was strong from delivering papers.
   b. She was older and taller than the other students.
   c. After years of teasing, she knew how to defend herself.
   d. Mr. Smart stayed in school with her to stop the teasing.

6. Based on the selection, which words *best* describe Mrs. Jordan?
   a. a stern, hard teacher
   b. a new teacher
   c. a caring teacher
   d. a polite teacher

7. What would be a good title for this selection?
   a. Detective Donna Brags Again
   b. Help for a New Student
   c. A Job Before School
   d. School Children Can Be Mean

51

B   **Answer the questions on the lines provided.**

1. When Nicky got to the school playground, why did he say he was going to look for a big brain?

   _____

   _____

2. Write a summary of the selection. Remember that a summary should include only the major points.

   _____

   _____

   _____

   _____

   _____

3. How does the art at the beginning of the selection help the reader understand the character named Joanne?

   _____

   _____

   _____

   _____

C   **Donna Chang says that to be a good detective you just need to watch carefully, listen carefully, and think. Complete the chart below with examples from the selection of these three detective skills that Donna uses.**

Detective Skill	Example(s)
Watch carefully	
Listen carefully	
Think	

D What are these expressions and words really saying? Match column *A* with column *B*. Write the letter of the correct meaning from column *B* next to each sentence in column *A*.

Column A

_____ 1. Liz was *the answer to any teachers dream.*

_____ 2. Donna was always *sizing up others.*

_____ 3. I was *on the warpath.*

_____ 4. Liz always *mothered* the new classmates.

_____ 5. Donna had put herself *out on a limb again.*

_____ 6. Nicky *interrupted* Liz's story several times.

_____ 7. Please come straight home. *Don't hang around* the play-ground.

_____ 8. The whole class was *amazed* at Donna's work.

_____ 9. Joanne began to *feel at home.*

_____ 10. Liz's eyes *grew wide.*

_____ 11. Joanne could not *find her way around.*

_____ 12. No one should *hurt her feelings.*

_____ 13. I *spotted* someone.

_____ 14. Tell us his *biography.*

Column B

a. took good care of; guarded

b. stared

c. very surprised

d. noticed

e. absent

f. ready to fight

g. know where everything was

h. broke into

i. life story

j. the kind of child an adult could depend on

k. stay longer than is necessary

l. studying people to try to understand them better

m. in a spot from which it would be hard to escape without embarrassment

n. was comfortable

o. insult her

53

E Liz's older brother Glenn is in the eighth grade. He is a reporter for the school newspaper. Glenn has written the following articles. Each one needs a headline. Help Glenn. Using the box below as a guide, write a headline for each article. One is done for you.

---

1. The headline should tell the main idea or topic of the article.

2. The headline is not written in sentence form. It is written as a phrase.

3. The important words in a headline start with a capital letter.

Boy Rewarded for Helping Cat

1. _____

Hugh Baldwin has proved that a kind heart can pay off. On November 3, Hugh found a cat lying in the street. The animal had a broken leg. Hugh was on his way to school, but he stopped to help.

He got some water for the cat. Then he sat by the cat waiting for passersby. At last, Mrs. Belle Silva of 3982 Bow Avenue saw them and stopped.

Mrs. Silva and Hugh took the cat to the veterinarian, where it was treated. While Hugh went on to school, the owner was located. Hugh received a reward of $25 from the cat's grateful master.

2. _____

One science class, in Room 603, has been raising tadpoles for the last three weeks. Lea Tolson, a fifth grader, found the frog eggs in a pond on Edgewood Avenue. The class has watched, fed, and learned from the tadpoles as they have hatched from the eggs.

For the Thanksgiving holiday, Lea offered to take the tadpoles home. Somehow, in her rush to start the vacation, she forgot them in the classroom.

The class was upset upon returning the following Monday morning to discover that most of the tadpoles had turned into frogs and gone their own ways.

That day, the science class changed into a frog hunt. It is reported that the creatures were found jumping about in the halls, the sinks, the waste cans, and the classrooms of the whole first floor. Dr. Lin, our principal, leaped fast to capture one frog in his desk drawer and another by his telephone. Maybe the frog was planning to order some flies for lunch.

© Houghton Mifflin Harcourt Publishing Company

3. _____

Fifth-grade students at Crest School are displaying what they made in art class this term. The art show will be held on June 7 in the auditorium. One lucky student will receive a trophy for "Best Artwork." The Parent-Teacher Association will be meeting that night. Many parents are expected to come to view the masterpieces created by their children. The art teachers have put on a beautiful show. The colorful pottery is gathering praise from all who have seen it arranged on one side of the room. Beautiful watercolor paintings are displayed on the stage. Puppets, weavings, and needlework are placed near the windows. Cutouts and dioramas are by the door.

Dr. Lin, the principal, has given permission for students to view the art every day after school from June 8 to June 23.

F **Read these sentences. Most of them belong in one paragraph. Label the sentence that tells the main idea with the letters *M.I.* Place a *D* next to the other sentences that are details supporting the main idea. Two sentences do not help the main idea or topic, so they do not belong. Label them *X*.**

_____ 1. Joanne rides her bike from door to door delivering papers early each morning.

_____ 2. Joanne likes to read the comics in the morning paper.

_____ 3. People complain if Joanne is careless and the paper lands in the bushes or on the roof. So Joanne puts each paper where it should go.

_____ 4. Joanne must go out every two weeks to collect money for the papers she has delivered.

_____ 5. Joanne does not have an easy job.

_____ 6. Newspapers give us much information on many topics.

_____ 7. At sunrise, a truck leaves a pile of papers at Joanne's door. She must fold them. They must be put into plastic bags on rainy days.

_____ 8. Because some of her customers live on the second floor, Joanne walks up many steps each day.

Selection 8

Early one Sunday morning, Loretta was awakened by the sound of a terrible crash on the steep hill near her grandmother's house.

"Guess what, Gran!" she said. "In our English class, we're putting out a school newspaper. Do you think I should go see what happened? It might be an interesting article for the newspaper."

"It sounded like a car accident," Grandmother remarked, "and it's the kind of news that papers will print."

All that evening, Loretta struggled to write a newspaper article. She wrote a headline that she felt gave a good idea of the contents of the story.

The next day on the school bus she read what she had written to some of her classmates.

Valerie exclaimed, "That's a great story! I enjoyed the excitement!"

"I felt as if I were right there in the pileup of cars," said Tyrone.

Loretta could hardly wait for the English lesson to begin. She raised her hand immediately to show Mr. Fedder, the teacher, her article. While the rest of the group worked on their projects, he studied it.

Loretta was bubbling over with excitement. "I hope you think it's good enough for our class newspaper, Mr. Fedder."

The teacher praised the fact that there were no spelling errors. "And the sentences all start with capital letters and end with periods," he complimented. "Good work, Loretta."

But his next words disappointed her.

"You'll have to make a few important changes," the teacher suggested. "This is going to be a newspaper story. You forgot what all newspaper stories should have."

Loretta studied her work. She read it again and again.

Ice Causes Pileup When
Truck Overturns

An unexpected drop in temperature after midnight caused ice to form on many roads. On steep Fleming Hill, several cars were stuck. As more cars slid down the hill, there was a giant pileup. The police should have closed the street, but they did not.

At 3:10 a.m., Lois Fant, driver of a large truck, started down the hill. Trying to stop the truck did not help. It joined the rest of the pileup, ending overturned across the road. That, finally, closed the road to traffic. It probably prevented even more accidents. The load on the truck, 8,500 cases of Foamy Soap, covered the road.

Then Loretta said, "Newspapers print all the facts. I have plenty of facts here."

"Indeed you do," agreed Mr. Fedder. "You have facts. But you have something else, too."

Then Loretta realized what he meant. "Some of the article is my own opinion!" she exclaimed. "Reporters should tell only facts!"

"Good thinking!" praised Mr. Fedder. "But I believe our class may need some work on telling the difference between facts and opinions."

The whole group discussed the differences for a while. They discovered the following:

---

1. A *fact* is a true piece of information. You must be able to prove your facts by showing where you found the information.

2. An *opinion* is what someone thinks about a topic. An opinion is not always a fact. This is because most people have different opinions about the same topic.

3. An opinion may be true, but it is still an opinion.

A Reread Loretta's newspaper article. Find the sentences that are opinions rather than facts. Write them here.

_____

_____

_____

_____

_____

_____

_____

_____

59

B **Read this short selection. Then complete the activities on pages 61–66.**

The next day, Mr. Fedder had a big box in class. It was wrapped in beautiful yellow and silver paper. The bow on top was dotted with small, yellow stars. The children gathered around it.

"Who gave you a present?" they asked.

"It's a gift for you, not for me!" their teacher said with a smile. "In this box are some very interesting topics. Each of you will pick one and look up information on it. When you've found out everything you can, write fifteen facts about your topic. Notice that I said facts. Please do not write opinions. The students who write few or no opinions will each find a surprise in this gift box three weeks from today!"

In great excitement, one at a time, the students went up to the box, closed their eyes, and pulled out a slip of paper. Then the shouting began.

The topics were things about which they had never heard! The students thought Mr. Fedder was fooling them.

"No, they're real!" he said. "If you knew what these things were, you would be able to write the facts without searching. The hunt is half the fun!"

Norman shouted, "Mine is something called *Ixora*!"

"That's all right," said Mr. Fedder. "Pick another."

In went Norman's hand again. Out it came! "*Kittiwake*!" he called. "That's worse than *Ixora*!"

"Do you want to try again?" inquired Mr. Fedder.

Norman shook his head. "I'd probably get one even worse."

For several days, the students hunted in dictionaries, in encyclopedias, on the computer, and in many indexes of books. They used all their study skills. They read and thought. Then they started to write facts.

On the following pages, you will find the research findings of a few of Mr. Fedder's topics and the notes the students took. Read both. Then pretend you are Mr. Fedder. On each page of notes, make a ✔ by every fact. Make an *X* by every opinion. Count all the checks. Write the number at the top of that page. If the student gets a score of 12 or more, she or he will get a surprise from the box.

Research Findings: The Kakapo

The kakapo is a very noisy bird of the parrot family. It is flightless, which means that it is unable to fly. The kakapo runs about on the ground. The birds have not flown for so many centuries that their wing muscles are tiny and weak.

The home of the kakapo is in a burrow under the ground. The birds move into holes that have been left by other animals. Throughout the day, the kakapos hide in their burrows.

As soon as it is dark, they crawl out, noisy and hungry. Their search for food continues until dawn. Their favorite food is the nectar of flowers. Kakapos locate the blossoms in the darkness by following the odor of the nectar.

Their brown feathers are arranged in a light and dark pattern that appears to be in stripes. This makes them very difficult to spot in the moonlight and shadows. Kakapos have beaks just like other parrots. However, around their bills are feathers that look like whiskers.

Very few kakapos remain. They are almost extinct because they taste good, and people have killed them for food. As more cities have spread out across the country, the animals that live with people have attacked the kakapos in their neighborhoods. The parrots are easy prey because they are unable to fly away.

Notes

Carmen Castillo _____

Kakapos

1. Kakapos are parrots that cannot fly.

2. They are almost extinct because humans like to eat them.

3. People should eat only vegetables to stop killing off many different kinds of animals.

4. Kakapos come out only at night to hunt for nectar in the flowers.

5. Rats, cats, and dogs destroy kakapos.

6. Kakapos live in burrows that other animals have dug.

7. The wing muscles of kakapos have gotten weak because they are not used.

8. Kakapos are very cute birds.

9. Human beings find it easy to kill kakapos. They could capture them instead and keep them as pets. That would keep many more kakapos alive, and they would not become extinct.

10. Kakapos find nectar in flowers at night by using their noses. They track the smell of the nectar until they find it.

11. Kakapos are noisy.

12. Kakapos hide in the daytime.

13. Kakapos have hooked beaks like parrots.

14. The striped, brown feathers make kakapos difficult to see at night.

15. Kakapos return to their burrows by sunrise.

Research Findings: The Guacharo

In South America, in the mountain caves along the coast lives a bird called guacharo or oilbird. It is found in Peru, Ecuador, Colombia, Venezuela, and Trinidad. For centuries the fat of the young guacharos has been boiled. From the boiled fat, humans obtain a clear, yellow, odorless oil. The people use it for lighting for their homes and for cooking.

The guacharo has large, blue eyes, short legs, weak feet, and a strong, yellow, hooked bill. When it spreads its wings, they stretch out to 36 inches. The color of the guacharo is reddish-brown, spotted with black and white. Around its mouth are long, stiff bristles.

The guacharo spends most of its life in darkness. As it flies around in dark caves, it gives off clicking sounds. Echoes come back to the guacharo. This helps the bird avoid bumping into anything that is in the way.

Deep in the caves, the guacharo builds its nest on ledges. In the saucer-shaped nest, the guacharo lays two, three, or four white eggs. Both parents take turns sitting on the eggs until they hatch.

At night the guacharo leaves the cave to get food. It eats the oily fruits of palms and laurels. It is the only fruit-eating bird in the world that flies at night.

Gwen King

My notes on Guacharos

1. Guacharos are birds found in South America.

2. People kill guacharos to get the fat they need for oil.

3. After removing the fat, people probably eat the guacharo because it looks good

    enough to eat.

4. The guacharo builds a saucer-shaped nest.

5. The guacharo likes to live in dark places, such as caves.

6. If there were enough guacharo birds in the world, the guacharo oil could be used

    in the motors of cars, trucks, ships, and planes.

7. The guacharo is a very attractive bird with beautiful, blue eyes.

8. People can only see the birds outside of caves during the night.

9. All echoes in areas where guacharos live probably come from

    sounds made by these birds.

10. The guacharo lays two to four white eggs.

11. The mother and father guacharos help take care of the eggs.

12. The guacharo likes to eat oily fruit.

13. The guacharo's wings can spread out to 36 inches.

14. The eyes of a guacharo are blue.

15. Some people use the oil from a guacharo to light their homes.

Research Findings: Quack Grass

In the United States and Canada, one of the worst plant pests is called quack grass. It also has several other names, such as devil's grass, witch grass, and quick grass. This weed was brought here from Europe, and it has been spreading rapidly ever since.

Quack grass is tall. It can be two, three, or four feet high. Under the ground lies the most serious cause of trouble. The roots form rhizomes. Rhizomes are strong, tough, horizontal roots that fan out in all directions. Leaves grow right on the rhizomes, come out above the soil and sprout new plants. In this way new patches of quack grass appear in different areas.

At the same time, the plant above the ground produces seeds. The seeds are spread by the breezes, by animals, and by birds. Many of the seeds start new quack grass plants, too. Once it forms, the quack grass chokes all the other neighboring plants. Farm crops and gardens have been destroyed by quack grass pushing them out.

It is difficult to get rid of quack grass. Digging it out does not work. If even a tiny part of the rhizome is left, it begins to sprout new plants. Poisons can kill it, but they can destroy other plantings, too.

Quack grass can be useful. Goats, sheep, and cattle are able to graze on it. On hills and on the banks of streams and rivers, the tough rhizomes of quack grass hold the soil more firmly in place to prevent it from washing away.

Notes

Alexander Lewis

Quack Grass

1. Quack grass is also called witchgrass.

2. All people hate quack grass.

3. The rhizomes are the roots of the quack grass.

4. The rhizomes spread horizontally under the ground. In this way, quack grass can pop out in different areas.

5. The rhizomes are hard and tough.

6. If the rhizomes are cut out, every bit of them must be removed.

7. If any part of the root is left in the ground, it can sprout new plants.

8. Cattle can use quack grass as food.

9. By spending much money on weed killers, the governments of the United States and Canada could destroy every bit of the quack grass. This would be good for farmers.

10. Quack grass is useful to hold the soil in place in hilly areas.

11. Quack grass is ugly.

12. Quack grass is a tall plant.

13. Quack grass keeps nearby plants from getting water and food from the soil. It chokes them out in this way.

14. Quack plants have stems, leaves, and seeds.

15. The seeds are scattered by the wind. They start new plants.

C **Choose a word to complete each sentence.**

prevent	immediately	rhizomes	approach
opinions	sprout	compliment	accident
article	rely	disappoint	errors
attractive	remark	steep	odor

1. A hill that is hard to climb is _____.

2. Mistakes are _____.

3. To say something is to _____.

4. Your thoughts about a subject are _____.

5. To come near is to _____.

6. To praise is to give a _____.

7. When a seed begins to grow, it starts to _____.

8. Tough, strong, horizontal roots are _____.

9. To stop something from happening is to _____.

10. To not do what is expected is to _____.

11. To do something right away is to do it _____.

12. To depend on is to _____.

13. A pretty scene is _____.

14. A wreck is an _____.

15. A story written for a newspaper is an _____.

Selection 9

An **outline** is a summary that lists the important information from a selection. Creating an outline is a good way to write down what you have read in your own words without copying many pages of information. Outlines can help you remember what you have read and learned.

Read this outline about a popular product. Then answer the questions in activity

A Popular Product—Chewing Gum

I. Used by ancient Greeks

   A. Chewed resin of mastic tree

   B. Gave us our word *masticate*, meaning **chew**

II. Used by the Wampanoag people in North America

   A. Chewed pieces of resin or sap from spruce trees

     1. Were tough to chew

     2. Tasted bad

   B. Introduced to the Pilgrims in 1600s

III. Began to spread in 1800s

   A. Introduction of spruce gum made with paraffin

     1. Introduced in Maine by John Curtis

     2. Introduced in 1848

   B. Discovery of the Osage people's chewing gum

     1. Discovered by pioneers settling the West

     2. Made of chicle, the sap of the Mexican sapodilla tree

C. Invention of chicle chewing gum with many flavors
   1. Invented by Thomas Adams
   2. First sold in the United States in 1870
   3. Made in popular flavors
      a. Licorice
      b. Cinnamon
      c. Clove
      d. Peppermint
      e. Spearmint

IV. Used throughout world in 1900s
  A. Growth of Wrigley Company
   1. Gum used across the United States
   2. Sold in stores
   3. Sold in vending machines

  B. Spread to other countries and continents
   1. Australia
   2. New Zealand
   3. Canada
   4. Europe
   5. Asia

  C. Growing sapodilla trees in Mexico
   1. Growing a tree for 60 to 70 years before getting chicle from it
   2. Collecting sap from a cut in the trunk of the sapodilla tree
   3. Selling sap or chicle to gum companies all over the world
   4. Becoming the main chicle exporting country in the world

  D. Trying to develop synthetic products to make chewing gum

  E. Invention of bubblegum in 1933

  F. Giving away baseball cards with chewing gum

  G. Invention of sugarless gum in 1940

A **Circle the correct answer to each question.**

1. What kind of information is in this outline?

   a. how bubblegum is made

   b. the ingredients in a stick of gum

   c. the history of chewing gum

   d. the most popular gum flavor

2. What is known about the use of gum in ancient times?

   a. It is mentioned in the Bible.

   b. It was discovered by the Romans.

   c. It was used in ancient Egypt.

   d. It was used in ancient Greece.

3. What is the title of the outline?

   a. Chewing Gum

   b. The History of Invention

   c. A Popular Product—Chewing Gum

   d. The World's Greatest Invention

4. The **main ideas** of an outline are shown by the use of Roman numbers. How many main ideas are in this outline?

   a. six   b. fifteen   c. fourteen   d. four

5. The **subtopics** are under the main ideas. They are shown by the use of capital letters. How many subtopics are under the third main idea?

   a. five   b. two   c. four   d. three

6. When did chewing gum begin to be used all over the world?

   a. in the 1800s

   b. in the 1900s

   c. in the 1600s

   d. during ancient times

7. Chicle is what part of the sapodilla tree?

   a. the bark

   b. the sap

   c. the leaf

   d. It is not part of it.

8. What did the ancient Greeks chew?

   a. chicle

   b. sap from the sapodilla tree

   c. resin from the spruce tree

   d. resin from the mastic tree

9. Why do you think chewing gum makers are trying to make gum from synthetic materials?

   a. Getting sap from sapodilla trees is dangerous work.

   b. There is a disease that is destroying many chicle trees in the world.

   c. The sapodilla trees in Mexico have become too old.

   d. It takes a long time for sapodilla trees to produce enough chicle.

Name _____   Date _____

B Outlines are one way to write down information in a shorter form. Graphs are another means of doing this. Graphs compare things. A graph shows a clear picture and is easy to understand. Here is some more information about chewing gum. It is shown on a circle graph. Read the graph and answer the questions.

Ingredients in Modern Chewing Gum

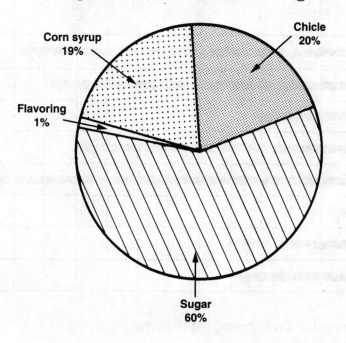

1. How many ingredients are in most kinds of modern chewing gum? _____

2. Name all the ingredients used in chewing gum.

   _____

3. Which ingredient is used most in making chewing gum? _____

4. Which ingredient is used least in making chewing gum? _____

5. Which ingredients are used in almost the same amount in making chewing gum?

   _____

6. Is there more chicle or more corn syrup in gum? _____

7. Is there less chicle or less sugar in gum? _____

8. What information does this circle graph show?

   _____

Selection 9
Core Skills Reading Comprehension, Grade 5

Name _____ Date _____

C Below is a bar graph. Read the information it contains and answer the questions.

Favorite Gum Flavors Among School Children

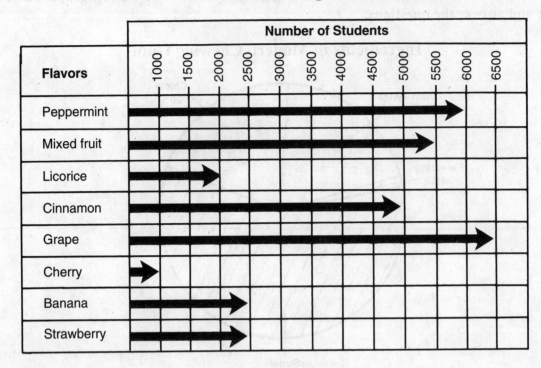

1. Which was the least popular flavor among the children?

   _____

2. Which was the most popular flavor? _____

3. Which two flavors were equally popular with the children?

   _____

4. About how many children chose cinnamon? _____

5. About how many children chose peppermint? _____

6. Did the children like mixed fruit or banana gum better?

   _____

7. Which was more popular, cinnamon or grape gum?

   _____

8. What information does this bar graph show?

   _____

   _____

72

D Read the bar graph and answer the following questions.

How Much Sugarless Gum Was Chewed in the World in 1980

	NUMBER OF PEOPLE											
	2500	3000	3500	4000	4500	5000	5500	6000	6500	7000	7500	8000
United States												
Germany												
Mexico												
France												
Russia												
Canada												
England												
Sweden												

1. How many people in England chewed sugarless gum? _____

2. Which country had the least number of sugarless gum chewers?

    _____

3. Which country used more sugarless gum, Sweden or Germany?

    _____

4. How many people in Mexico chewed sugarless gum? _____

5. How many more people chewed sugarless gum in France than in Sweden?

    _____

6. In what countries did people chew the same amount of sugarless gum?

    _____

7. How many fewer Canadians chewed sugarless gum than people in the United States?

    _____

8. What information does this bar graph show?

    _____

73

Selection 10

After you have located information, you usually have a jumble of facts. You can put these facts in an outline under different topics. Once the information is outlined, it is easy to find any fact quickly.

An outline is a shorter way of writing and remembering information. Only main ideas and important details are included. Here is a form that should be used to outline material.

_____ (The **title** explains the topic of the selection.)

(This is the **main idea** of the paragraph. Main ideas use Roman numerals.)

I.
 A.
 B.   (These are the supporting details
 C.   of the same paragraph. They are
 D.   called **subtopics**.)

(This is the main idea of the second paragraph.)

II.
 A.
 B.   (Subtopics use capital letters.)
 C.

(This is the main idea of the third paragraph.)

III.
 A.
 B.
 C.
  1.   (These are additional **details** for
  2.   subtopic C. These use Arabic
       numbers.)

A Read this selection. Think of how you would outline the information. Then complete the outline.

The Linnaea, or twinflower, is a beautiful plant. It is an evergreen, so it does not lose its leaves in the winter. It has long, woody stems. The leaves are round, and the flowers are shaped like bells. They can be either pink or white. A sweet, pleasant odor is given off by the pretty blossoms.

The twinflower is found only in a few places. It grows in North America, in Sweden and Norway, and in some parts of Asia. It requires loose, damp soil.

It is easy to grow Linnaeas. Just cut off a section of the stem. Put it in some water. Wait a few days until roots form. Then plant it in some soft, fine soil. Water it often.

Name _____ Date _____

_____ (Title)

I. _____

    A. Is an evergreen
        1. Stays green all winter
        2. Does not lose its leaves in the cold
    B. Has long, woody stems
    C. Has round leaves
    D. Has bell-shaped flowers
    E. Has white or pink blossoms
    F. Gives off a sweet, pleasant odor

II. _____

    A. Grows in North America
    B. Grows in Norway and Sweden
    C. Grows in Asia
    D. Requires loose, damp soil

III. _____

    A. Cut off part of stem.
    B. Place in water.
    C. Wait for roots to grow.
    D. Plant in right kind of soil.
    E. Water often.

B Read this selection. Then complete the outline with the information you have read.

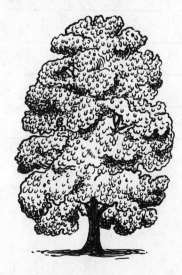

The tulip tree, or tulip poplar, is outstanding in appearance. It is the tallest broadleaf tree found in the eastern United States. It can grow two hundred feet high. Its trunk can be as wide as a car is long. The beautiful, yellow blossoms look like tulips. Its long-stemmed, smooth, graceful leaves are notched. The outer wood, or the bark, of the tree is white. The inner wood is a pretty shade of yellow.

The tulip poplar is found only in North America. The tree grows in the eastern United States from Maine to Florida. It also grows as far west as Arkansas. This tree is the state tree of Tennessee, Kentucky, and Indiana, so of course it is found in these states, too.

75

The tulip tree has several uses. It produces hard wood that is very valuable. Expensive furniture is made from it. The tulip poplar is used to make beautiful baskets, boxes, and ornaments, too.

_____ (Title)

I. Is outstanding in appearance _____

    A. _____

    B. _____

    C. _____

    D. _____

    E. _____

    F. _____

    G. _____

II. Is found only in North America _____

    A. _____

    B. _____

    C. Is the state tree of three states _____

        1. _____

        2. _____

        3. _____

III. Has several uses _____

    A. _____

    B. _____

    C. _____

    D. _____

Name _____ Date _____

C Read this selection about an odd animal. Prepare a complete outline from what you read. If you look back at the sample outlines, you will find it easy to write your own outline.

The tailorbird has unusual nesting habits. It starts to build a nest by putting two broad leaves together. It uses its sharp beak to stab holes in the edges of the leaves. Then it uses a spider web as thread to sew the leaves together. The nest it makes is like a sack with an open top. The tailorbird lines its nest to make the baby birds comfortable. To do this, it uses silky threads from plants, soft grass, or animal hairs. The nest is hidden in thick bushes. Two or three speckled eggs are laid in a nest.

The tailorbird looks unusual, too. It is only four to six inches long. Its bill is very thin and sharp. Its head is red. The back of the tailorbird is olive green, but its front is light gray. Its long tail sticks up straight in the air.

Tailorbirds are found in few places. They live only in areas that have been settled and cleared by people. They make homes in gardens and on farms. They can be seen in India, the East Indies, and the Philippine Islands.

_____ (Title)

I. _____

   A. _____

      1. _____

      2. _____

   B. _____

   C. _____

      1. _____

      2. _____

      3. _____

   D. _____

   E. _____

Selection 10
Core Skills Reading Comprehension, Grade 5

Name _____ Date _____

II. _____

    A. _____

    B. _____

    C. _____

    D. _____

    E. _____

III. _____

    A. _____

    B. _____

    C. _____

Name _____ Date _____

D Study the outline below. Then label the parts marked by stars. Use the labels from the box.

a. Additional details for subtopics	**c.** Title
b. Subtopics	**d.** Main idea

The Brown Pelican ✱ 1. _____

I. Where found

   A. On the warmer parts of the east and west coasts of the United States

   B. On the east and west coasts of Central America

   C. On the east and west coasts halfway down South America

   ✱ 2. _____

II. Nesting habits ✱ 3. _____

   A. Choosing of nesting site by males

   B. Finding a mate

   C. Searching for nest materials by males

     1. Sticks   4. Leaves

     2. Straw   5. Grass

     3. Reeds

   ✱ 4. _____

   D. Building of nest by females

   E. Laying two or three eggs

   F. Sitting on eggs by both parents

   ✱ 5. _____

   G. Shading of the naked chicks from the sun by both parents

   H. Feeding of babies by both parents

   ✱ 6. _____

III. Fishing habits ✱ 7. _____

   A. Catch fish in pouch under bill

   B. Catch fish under the water

   C. Catch many fish easily

   ✱ 8. _____

79

E **Circle the correct answer to each question.**

1. Why must pelican parents shade their babies?

   a. Baby pelican chicks will not eat when it is sunny.

   b. Baby pelicans are not covered with feathers.

   c. The parents must keep the rain off the babies.

   d. The babies must be protected from wild animals.

2. How do tailorbirds sew their nests together?

   a. with a needle and thread

   b. with their beaks and cotton thread

   c. with stones and animal hairs

   d. with their beaks and spider web threads

3. What is true about tailorbirds?

   a. They like to live in the crowded jungle.

   b. They live mostly in cities.

   c. They live where people live.

   d. They live far away from human beings.

4. Where are tailorbirds found?

   a. South America

   b. the United States

   c. India

   d. Antarctica

5. What statement is true about the Linnaea?

   a. It keeps its leaves in winter.

   b. It loses its leaves in cold weather.

   c. It gives off a bad odor.

   d. It is hard to grow.

6. For what is the tulip poplar used?

   a. Its flowers are used as food for humans.

   b. People eat its leaves.

   c. The roots are used in medicine.

   d. Its wood makes good furniture.

7. If a tailorbird is measured against a 12-inch ruler, what is true?

   a. It is longer than the ruler.

   b. It is a yard long.

   c. It is shorter than the ruler.

   d. It is about as long as the ruler.

8. How do pelicans catch fish?

   a. in their pouches

   b. from fishermen's nets

   c. with their webbed feet

   d. from fishermen's lines

F Write the correct word to complete each sentence.

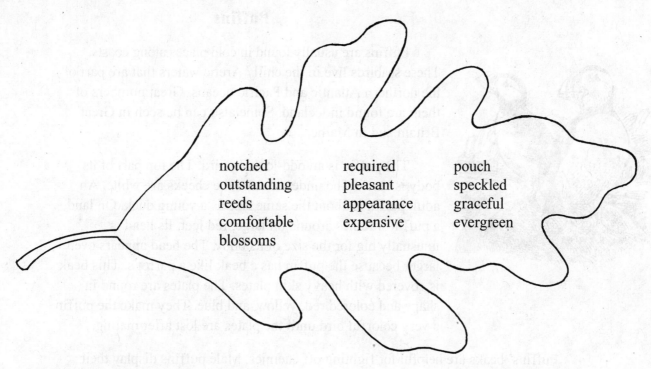

notched   required   pouch
outstanding pleasant   speckled
reeds   appearance   graceful
comfortable expensive   evergreen
blossoms

1. To come out on a stage is to make an _____.

2. Something covered with small spots is _____.

3. If the sofa is soft and wide, it is probably _____.

4. To be a dancer, a person must be _____.

5. A friendly person is usually _____.

6. If boots cost a lot of money, they are _____.

7. A _____ is a kind of small bag.

8. Around most ponds, tall, slender _____ can be found.

9. Another word for "flowers" is _____.

10. Pines and spruces are called _____ trees.

11. If you have read the stories and know the definitions of all these words, you have done an

    _____ job.

12. The leaf in this picture is _____.

Selection 11

Puffins

Puffins are usually found in cold places along coasts. These seabirds live in the chilly Arctic waters that are part of the northern Atlantic and Pacific oceans. Great numbers of them are found in Iceland. Some also can be seen in Great Britain and in Maine.

The puffin is an odd-looking bird. The top part of its body is black. The underside and the cheeks are white. An adult puffin is about the same size as a young duck. On land, a puffin waddles around on large, red feet. Its head is unusually big for the size of its body. The head appears even larger because the puffin has a beak like a parrot's. This beak is covered with heavy skin plates. The plates are round in shape and colored red, yellow, and blue. They make the puffin a very colorful bird until the plates are lost after mating.

Puffins' beaks are helpful for fighting off enemies. Male puffins display their bills to attract a mate. These birds show they love each other by rubbing beaks together. During nesting time, the beak acts as a shovel to dig a hole in a patch of soft earth on the rocks. An egg is laid in the hole. When carrying food to baby birds, the parents' beaks double as cups and spoons. A puffin's beak is a useful tool.

The puffin is an expert fisher. It catches different kinds of sea animals, such as smelt, herring, and shrimp. The puffin's beak can hold as many as ten fish to feed the family.

A **Prepare an outline from what you read about puffins. Include the title, main ideas, subtopics, and details under some of the subtopics.**

_____ (Title)

I. ___Where puffins are found_____

    A. _____

    B. _____

    C. _____

    D. _____

II. _____

   A. _____

   B. _____

   C. _____

   D. _____

   E. _____

   F. _____

      1. _____

      2. _____

      3. _____

      4. _____

III. _____

   A. _____

   B. _____

   C. _____

   D. _____

IV. _____

   A. _____

   B. _____

Name _____ Date _____

B Below is a graph that shows a comparison. Gulls and puffins nest on the same rocky pieces of
land in cold Arctic areas. The gulls often attack the puffins' nests to eat the eggs or the babies.
People who study birds are afraid that in the future the gulls may kill off most of the puffins.
A scientist has been keeping track of the number of puffins compared to the number of gulls in
the Arctic regions. Study this line graph. You will find much information in a small space. Then
answer the questions.

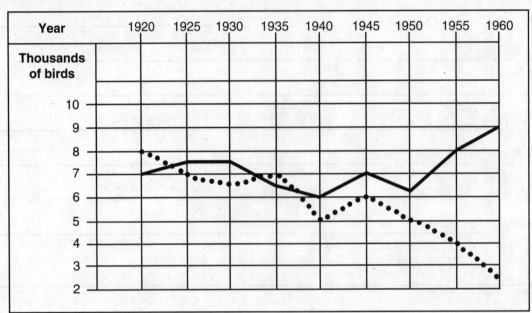

Puffins are represented by ●●●●●●●●●   Gulls are represented by ━━━━━━━

1. Which bird had the highest population in 1960? _____

2. When were there more puffins than gulls? Write all the years. _____

3. In what year was the population of gulls the lowest? _____

4. In what year was the puffin population the lowest? _____

5. In what years did the gull population remain the same? _____

6. In 1940, how many gulls were in the Arctic region? _____

7. In 1940, how many puffins were there? _____

8. How many gulls were there in 1950? _____

9. In 1940, how did the number of puffins compare to the number of gulls?

_____

_____

Name _____ Date _____

C Study the picture graph below. Use the graph to answer the questions.

Different Species of Birds Found in North America, Europe, and India
United States (including Hawaii and Alaska)
Mexico
Canada
Europe
India

Each stands for 40 species.

1. One whole bird on the graph stands for _____ species.

2. Four whole birds on the graph stand for _____ species.

3. Half of a bird on the graph stands for _____ species.

4. Five and one-half birds on the graph stand for _____ species.

5. Where were most species found? _____

6. About how many were found there? _____

7. Where were the fewest species found? _____

8. How many species of birds were found in Mexico? _____

9. There were 580 species found in _____.

10. How many species of birds were found in the United States? _____

11. How many more species were found in India than in Mexico? _____

12. How many fewer species of birds were found in the United States than in India? _____

Selection 11
Core Skills Reading Comprehension, Grade 5

Name _____ Date _____

D Here is a circle graph explaining which kinds of fish were the most popular foods of puffins living in zoos in Great Britain. Study the graph and use it to answer the questions.

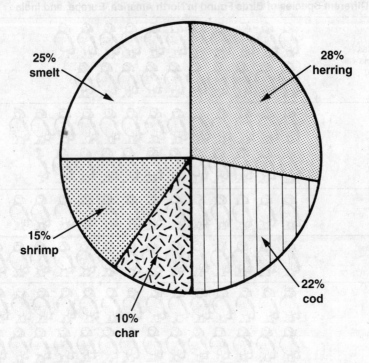

1. Which fish did puffins eat the least? _____

2. Which fish did puffins eat the most? _____

3. Did they eat more smelt or cod? _____

4. Which two kinds of fish together made up half of what the puffins ate?

   _____   _____

5. Half of the circle equals _____ percent.

6. Did the puffins eat fewer shrimp or fewer char? _____

7. Did the puffins eat more shrimp or more cod? _____

8. Which was the second most popular kind of fish? _____

9. Which two kinds of fish together made up 25% of what the puffins ate?

   _____   _____

10. Where did the people who made the graph study puffins? _____

   _____

Skills Review: Selections 7–11

A Outlines help us put large amounts of reading material into fewer words. Outlines also help us remember important facts in selections. Study the following outline carefully and then answer the questions.

Poisonous Sea Animals

I. Crown of thorns starfish
  A. Attacks only to defend itself
  B. Uses spines
    1. Has spines covered with venom
    2. Causes painful puncture wounds with spines

II. Stingray
  A. Tries to avoid enemies
    1. Lies hidden in sand
    2. Moves away slowly
  B. Uses barbed stingers for defense
    1. Are hidden in tail
    2. Hurt enemy
    3. Push deep into enemies
    4. Leave venom in wounds

III. Stonefish
  A. Blends in with natural surroundings
    1. Found deep in soft sand, algae, or coral
    2. Stays hidden from human and sea enemies
  B. Attacks enemies
    1. Waits for enemies to come close
    2. Uses dorsal fin to jab enemies
  C. Has poisonous venom
    1. Makes victim unconscious
    2. May cause paralysis or death

1. How many subtopics are under main idea II? Circle the correct answer.

  a. four   **c.** five

  b. three   **d.** two

2. How many main ideas are in the outline? Circle the correct answer.

  a. two   **c.** four

  b. three   **d.** five

3. What information is under main idea III, subtopic B, additional information number 2?

   _____

4. What did you learn about the sea animals in this outline?

   _____

   _____

5. What can happen to a person if attacked by a stonefish?

   _____

   _____

6. How does the stingray avoid its enemy?

   _____

7. What information is under main idea I, subtopic A?

   _____

8. What kind of animal is the crown of thorns? _____

9. Where is the venom stored in the crown of thorns? _____

10. Where is the venom of the stingray stored? _____

11. What does the stonefish use to jab enemies? _____

12. Where are the stingray's barbed stingers hidden? _____

13. What information is under main idea II, subtopic B?

   _____

14. What information is under main idea III, subtopic C, additional information 2?

   _____

   _____

B **Choose words from the box to complete the crossword puzzle on the next page.**

amazed	dependable	masticate	quit	sprout
adult	disappointed	relief	squirm	cap
fizz	popular	rely	trophy	chicle
resin	tune			

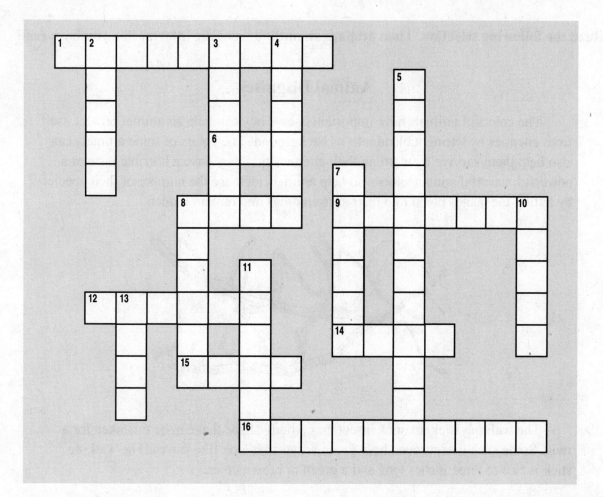

Across

1. to chew

6. something for the head

8. to depend on

9. well-liked

12. to wiggle

14. a song

15. to bubble

16. trustworthy

Down

2. a grownup

3. what makes gum chewy

4. a prize; a silver cup

5. did not get what was expected

7. to grow from a seed

8. comfort; a better feeling

10. sap of a spruce tree

11. very surprised

13. to stop doing something

89

C **Read the following selection. Then prepare an outline from the information you have read.**

Animal Disguises

The colors of animals have important uses. They can help an animal protect itself from enemies by letting it blend into its background. The colors of some animals can also help them survive by warning their enemies that they have a horrible taste or a powerful, harmful sting. Colors also help animals increase the number of their species by letting the babies blend into their surroundings and remain hidden.

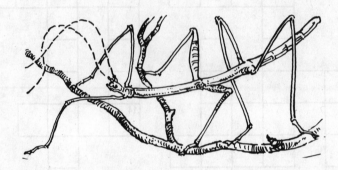

The walking stick, or stick insect, has a body shape that can be mistaken for a twig. Some stick insects even have green wings that look like leaves. The walking stick is two to three inches long and a green or brown color.

There is an unusual fish found in the Amazon that looks like a dead leaf. Its transparent, small fins help it move unnoticed to get close to its food—smaller fish. If the Amazon fish gets caught in a net, it lies flat and remains still, looking like a dead leaf. Usually, it is tossed back into the water.

There is a small toad found in South America that also resembles a leaf. This flat toad has a sharp snout like the pointed end of a leaf. On its green back, it even has a vein down the middle like the midrib of a leaf. Two small black spots on this toad could easily be mistaken for holes in a leaf that has fallen from a tree.

_____ (Title)

I. Uses of animal body colors _____

    A. _____

    B. _____

    C. _____

II. Walking stick _____

    A. _____

    B. _____

    C. _____

    D. _____

III. _____

    A. Transparent, small fins unnoticed as it nears prey

    B. _____

    C. _____

IV. _____

    A. _____

    B. Vein like a midrib of a leaf

    C. _____

Name _____ Date _____

D Professor Cambria and Professor Yang made a study of venomous sea animals. They put their findings on a graph. Study the graph and then answer the questions.

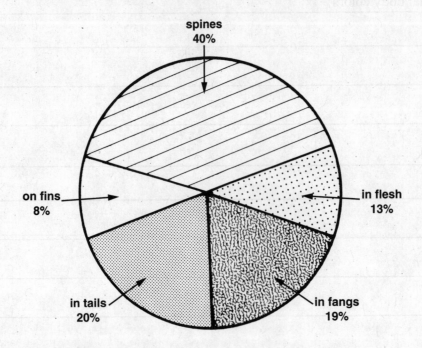

1. In which place does the greatest number of sea animals store venom? _____

2. In which two places do almost the same number of sea animals store venom?

   _____

3. Which is the least used place to store venom? _____

4. What percentage does the whole circle represent? _____

5. What percentage of sea creatures store venom in their flesh? _____

6. What do you know about 40 percent of these sea animals?

   _____

7. How much greater is the number of sea animals that have spines covered with venom than those that store venom in their tails?

   _____

8. What information does this graph show?

   _____

Selection 12

The Uncertain Pianist

Characters

Rachel, an eleven-year-old girl
Dad, Rachel's father

(As the curtain rises, Rachel is seated at a piano in her living room, playing a song from a music book. Several times she starts and stops, sighing, after playing wrong notes. Finally, she bangs the keys with both hands.)

Rachel: I hate this boring song!

(Rachel stares at the book. Half a minute later, Dad enters the living room.)

Dad: The music stopped. I thought you might have fallen asleep. *(He smiles at his own joke.)*

Rachel: *(lowering her head)* I just don't feel like playing this evening.

Dad: *(sitting next to Rachel)* It seems as though you haven't really felt like playing the piano for a while. I can hear that in the sounds that come from the keys. What's changed, Rachel? You used to enjoy the piano so much.

Rachel: *(with her head still lowered)* The songs I'm playing are as boring as dirt.

Dad: Then tell your teacher you'd like to try some new music.

Rachel: *(takes a deep breath and looks at Dad)* I guess it's not the music. It's . . . it's just that . . . I'll never be as good as you. You don't have to stop and check that your fingers are on the right keys. Your fingers sweep across them, perfectly hitting every note. . . . Dad, I'll never be like you—giving concerts all over the country where hundreds of people go hear you play. *(Her voice grows angry.)* It's hopeless. So why should I keep practicing?

Dad: *(frowning)* The most important reason to play the piano is because you enjoy it. If playing is no fun, then you shouldn't do it. *(He voice grows gentle.)* But you shouldn't stop playing because you don't think you'll ever be good enough. Who knows how good you can be?

93

Rachel: *(still doubtful)* I don't know, Dad.

(Dad jumps up from the piano bench and chooses a book from several on the top of the piano.)

Dad: I have an idea. Don't practice your regular music today. Instead, let's play a duet. As usual, you play the part for the left hand, and I'll play the part for the right hand.

Rachel: *(smiling)* Okay! You know how much I like to play duets with you.

(Rachel and Dad play a short duet with great energy.)

Rachel: *(with a laugh)* That was so much fun!

Dad: I'm impressed with how well you played your part. Rachel, you do have a lot of talent. *(looking at his watch)* Uh-oh. It's already six o'clock. Want to help me cook dinner?

Rachel: Can I come in a while? Right now I'd like to practice a little longer.

Dad: *(smiling)* Sure.

(Dad leaves the room. Rachel opens her music book and starts playing a cheerful song. The curtain falls.)

A **Circle the correct answer for each question.**

1. What is the last thing Rachel did during the action of the play?
   a. watched her father play the piano
   b. practiced the piano more
   c. cooked dinner
   d. played a duet

2. Read the stage instructions at the beginning of the play. (They begin with *"As the curtain rises,"*.) What do these instructions show about Rachel?
   a. She feels lonely.
   b. She feels sad.
   c. She feels frustrated.
   d. She feels worried.

3. Which of these sentences from the play tells you that Rachel and her father had played duets before?
   a. *"It seems as though you haven't really felt like playing the piano for a while."* (Dad)
   b. *"You used to enjoy the piano so much."* (Dad)
   c. *"You know how much I like to play duets with you."* (Rachel)
   d. *"Right now I'd like to practice a little longer."* (Rachel)

4. How did Rachel's father help her to solve her problem?

   a. He told her she could do other activities if she preferred.

   b. He helped her understand that sometimes piano music is boring.

   c. He told her she could be a concert pianist someday.

   d. He helped her realize that she enjoyed playing the piano.

5. Which of these lines from the play expresses a main theme?

   a. *"Then tell your teacher you'd like to try some new music."* (Dad)

   b. *"The most important reason to play the piano is because you enjoy it."* (Dad)

   c. *"Dad, I'll never be like you—giving concerts all over the country where hundreds of people go hear you play."* (Rachel)

   d. *"I hate this boring song!"* (Rachel)

6. Based on the play, how does Rachel feel about her father?

   a. She greatly admires her father.

   b. She resents her father's success.

   c. She wants to play better than her father.

   d. She thinks her father expects too much from her.

7. Based on things that Rachel's father says in the play, which of these statements about him is *most likely* true?

   a. He wants Rachel to get along with her teacher better.

   b. He wants Rachel to practice more hours each day.

   c. He wants Rachel to do things she enjoys doing.

   d. He wants Rachel to be a concert pianist one day.

B **Answer the questions on the lines provided.**

1. Why does Rachel tell her father that the songs she is playing are boring?

   _____

   _____

   _____

2. Why does Rachel mention dirt to her father?

   _____

   _____

   _____

3. Describe the sounds coming from the piano at the beginning of the play and at the very end of the play. Then tell what this shows about Rachel.

_____

_____

_____

_____

4. Describe how Rachel changes from the beginning to the end of the play.

_____

_____

_____

_____

C In a Venn diagram, you can compare and contrast two persons, things, events, or ideas. Use this Venn diagram to compare and contrast Rachel and Dad at the beginning of the play. In the left circle, write one thing about Dad that is different from Rachel. In the right circle, write one thing about Rachel that is different from Dad. In the area where the two circles overlap, write one thing that is the same about Dad and Rachel.

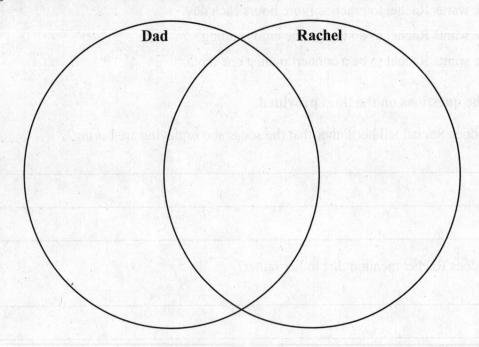

Dad   Rachel

Name _____ Date _____

D Some words have more than one meaning. Read the dictionary entry then answer questions 1–2.

> **note** (nōt) *n* 1: a short informal letter 2: a brief comment
>   3: a written symbol used in music *v* 1: to notice carefully
>   2: to record in writing

1. How many different meanings of *note* are shown in the dictionary entry?

_____

2. Which meaning of *note* is used in "The Uncertain Pianist"? Write the definition.

_____

3. Decide the meaning of the underlined word in the sentence below.

> The key to success is hard work.

Then circle the letter of the sentence in which *key* has the same meaning as it does in the sentence above.

a. The key to the front door is lost.

b. One piano key doesn't work.

c. The answer key is at the back of the book.

d. Being grateful for what you have is one key to happiness.

Selection 13

Measuring the Rain

You will need:

- glass or plastic container, with a flat bottom and straight sides, that is at least 5 inches high
- small funnel
- strip of paper 2 inches wide and 5 inches high
- ruler
- waterproof marker
- clear packing tape
- notebook
- pencil

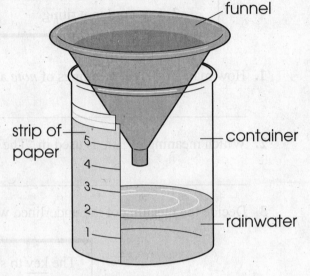

What to do:

1. Make a scale for your rain **gauge**. First, cut a strip of paper about 2 inches wide and 5 inches high. Then, use the ruler and the waterproof marker to make 1-inch marks, from 1 to 5, on the strip of paper. (See the diagram.)

2. First, attach the paper to a glass or plastic container with clear packing tape. The 1-inch mark should be at the bottom of the container; the 5-inch mark should be at the top. Then be sure to completely cover the scale with tape to keep it from getting wet. Finally, set the funnel inside the container. (See the diagram.)

3. Place your rain gauge on a level surface in an open area that is clear of buildings, tree branches, and sprinklers.

4. Check the gauge each day at the same time. Use the scale on the side of the container to determine the number of inches of rainfall.

5. Record the amount of new rainfall in your notebook along with the date and time of day.

6. After you record the information each day, pour out the water in the container so that the gauge will be ready for the next rainfall.

7. When you have measured rainfall for one month, add up all of the daily totals in your notebook. Then divide that number by the number of days you took measurements. Record the result in your notebook.

What is the result?

   You divide the sum of the daily totals for the month by the number of days you took measurements. The answer shows the average number of inches of rainfall per day for that month.

What does a rain gauge do?

Rain gauges measure the amount of rain that falls during a certain period of time. Water collects in the gauge when there is enough rainfall to measure.

Most rain gauges collect water in a storage container, and a scale or ruler measures the amount of rainfall. Some more complicated gauges weigh the water. One method of measuring rainfall involves the use of radar. Radio waves are reflected, or echoed, by raindrops. These echoes look like spots of light on a radar screen. Bright spots mean large raindrops, paler spots mean small raindrops. This method is particularly useful for very small amounts of rain that other gauges miss.

Why measure rainfall?

Scientists measure rainfall with rain gauges in thousands of places around the world. They use the measurements to help calculate the average daily, monthly, and yearly amounts of rain in each region. Once scientists have figured out the averages, they can see patterns of rainfall over time in a specific area or note differences among regions. Understanding rainfall patterns helps many people. For example, farmers rely on this knowledge to plan irrigation for crops. Scientists record rainfall patterns for many reasons. They want to know more about weather changes in different parts of the world, and they try to understand how dangerous storms develop.

Total average rainfall for the whole world is about 34 inches a year, but the amount differs from place to place. Mount Waialeale, in the state of Hawaii, has an annual average rainfall of 460 inches, the highest in the world. The lowest annual average rainfall in the world was recorded in Arica, Chile, at less than 1 inch.

Who made the first rain gauge?

Historians think the first rain gauge was invented in about 1441 in what is now the country of Korea.Two hundred years later, Christopher Wren invented a tipping bucket rain gauge in England.

---

complicated (KOM plih KAY tehd) — not easy to understand

funnel — a cone-shaped tool with a thin tube at the top; used to pass liquids or solids into containers with small openings

gauge (gayj) — an instrument for measuring

radar (RAY dahr) — device used to find out distance, direction, and speed of unseen objects by the use of waves that reflect off their surfaces

---

Name _____ Date _____

A Circle the correct answer for each question.

1. In which of these places does the highest average yearly rainfall in the world occur?

   a. Chile

   b. England

   c. Korea

   d. Hawaii

2. Read this sentence, located in the first paragraph under "Why measure rainfall?" It is about something that scientists do.

   > They use the measurements to help calculate the average daily, monthly, and yearly amounts of rain in each region.

   Which words in this paragraph help the reader understand what *calculate* means?

   a. *rain gauges*

   b. *a specific area*

   c. *figured out*

   d. *differences among regions*

3. Read this detail from the selection, located in the first paragraph under "Why measure rainfall?" It is about something that scientists do.

   > [T]hey try to understand how dangerous storms develop.

   Which idea found in the selection is **best** supported by this detail?

   a. Scientists record rainfall patterns for many reasons.

   b. Using average rainfall amounts helps scientists see patterns of rainfall over time in a specific area.

   c. Farmers rely on rainfall patterns to plan irrigation for their crops.

   d. Scientists use rainfall measurements to help calculate average amounts of rain in an area.

4. The author asks a question in each heading **most likely** to

   a. keep the reader interested in the selection.

   b. encourage the reader to write down answers.

   c. show the reader the importance of rain gauges.

   d. help the reader better understand the directions.

100

5. Which sentence **best** tells about the main idea of the selection?

   a. Rain gauges are placed in thousands of places around the world to record regional rainfall patterns.

   b. Rain gauges measure water three different ways: by collecting it, by weighing it, and by using radar.

   c. Rain gauges can be made from simple materials and are used to understand weather patterns.

   d. Rain gauges may have been invented centuries ago in what is now the country of Korea.

6. According to the diagram, which must be true about the container used to make a rain gauge?

   a. It must be no more than 5 inches tall so that measurements are accurate.

   b. It must be wider than the funnel so that the gauge can catch the rain.

   c. It must be made of clear material so that the water level can be seen.

   d. It must have very thick sides so that the wind does not blow it over.

B A flow chart is a diagram that shows the steps in a process. The first step goes in the top box; the last step goes in the bottom box, and the steps in between go in the boxes in the middle. Using information from the selection, complete the flow chart below by filling in the missing steps for making a rain gauge.

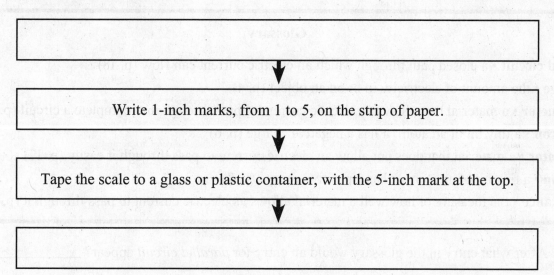

Write 1-inch marks, from 1 to 5, on the strip of paper.

Tape the scale to a glass or plastic container, with the 5-inch mark at the top.

The box after "Measuring the Rain" tells you the definitions of words in the selection that might be difficult or unfamiliar for readers. A **glossary** serves the same purpose for a book or other type of written work.

1. A glossary is a list of the definitions of words that appear in a book or other type of written work.

2. Not all the words in the written work are in the glossary—only the words that may be difficult or unfamiliar to many readers.

3. A glossary is usually at the end of a book.

4. Just like a dictionary, the words in a glossary are arranged in alphabetical order.

5. The pronunciation of words may or may not be included in a glossary.

6. Unlike a dictionary, if a word in the written work has more than one meaning, not all of them are given. Instead, only the meaning or meanings used in the written work are given.

7. Some glossaries include the numbers of the pages on which the words are used for the first time. Others glossaries do not.

C Study the portion of a glossary from a book for children titled *All About Electricity*. Then answer the questions.

Glossary

closed circuit • a closed path through which an electric current can flow (p. 18)

charge • the amount of electricity in or on an object (p. 4)

conductor • a material that allows an electric current to pass through it to complete a circuit (p. 11)

electron • a tiny bit of an atom; it has a negative charge (p. 6)

insulator • a material that does not allow an electric current to pass through it easily (p. 12)

proton • a tiny bit of an atom; it has a positive charge (p. 7)

resistance • the measure of how well a material allows an electric current to pass through it (p. 13)

1. After what entry in the glossary would an entry for *parallel circuit* appear? _____

2. On which page does the word *charge* first appear in the book? _____

3. The word *conductor* is first used in the book on page _____.

4. Which two words define things that are "a small part of an atom"?

   _____

5. Does the word *shock* appear in the book? _____

6. There is an error in the order of the words. How should this error be corrected?

   _____

You learned how you can measure the rain. Now read a poem about the rain and other things that happen during a rainstorm.

The Rainstorm

The air grows cool.
The sun vanishes.
The clouds advance. Brilliant colors
weave together on Earth's ceiling.
Blue, red, yellow, orange.

The thunder bellows[1].
The leaves rustle.
The wind whistles.
A colossal orchestra
plays its music in Earth's hall.
Rumble, whoosh, hiss, howl.

The clouds unlock.
The water cascades[2] down.
A massive shower
gently cleanses Earth's floor.
Drip, drop, splish, splash.

I dance playfully through the puddles.
I sing along with the symphony's song.
I taste the sweet drops of rain,
a joyous spectator[3]
to nature's majestic performance.
Applause, applause, applause.

[1] makes a loud, deep, roaring sound
[2] flows or pours like a waterfall
[3] a person who watches an event

D Circle the correct answer for each question.

1. The speaker of the poem compares Earth to

    a. an orchestra.

    b. a building.

    c. a waterfall.

    d. a rainstorm.

2. Which two stanzas, or sections, of the poem does the picture best illustrate?

    a. stanza 1 and stanza 2

    b. stanza 1 and stanza 4

    c. stanza 2 and stanza 3

    d. stanza 3 and stanza 4

3. Which of these *best* describes the structure of the poem?

    a. in the order in which the events would happen during a rainstorm

    b. in a series of causes and effects that the speaker finds interesting

    c. to show what is least important to most important about the rainstorm for the speaker

    d. to show what is most important to least important about the rainstorm for the speaker

E **Answer the questions on the lines provided.**

1. What do the second and third stanzas end with?

    _____

2. How does the speaker feel about the rainstorm? Name at least two details from the poem that support your answer.

    _____

    _____

F **The five senses are *sight, smell, taste, touch,* and *hearing*. Through which three senses does the speaker mainly experience the rainstorm? Complete the chart. Name the senses, the stanza (or stanzas) that is mostly about this sense, and examples of what the speaker experiences through this sense. The first sense has been started for you.**

Sense	Stanza(s)	Examples
Taste	4	
_____	___	_____
	___	_____
_____	___	_____
	___	_____

Selection 14

We're back! The detective team of Donna and Nicky is here to solve another mystery. Our latest case involved our father's friend Lester Judd. We went to visit him recently, and he told us this puzzling tale.

A few months ago in England, an unexpected discovery had been made. While cleaning out the attic of an ancient house, someone had found a secret closet in the wall. About a hundred early photographs were found in it. They had been taken and dated in 1860 and 1861 by a man named Archer. Dad said that Mr. Archer had been an important person in the early history of photography. People had written about him in books, encyclopedias, and newspapers.

Experts had examined the paper, the chemicals, and the kinds of negatives used. As far as they could tell, everything was what the early photographers had used in the 1860s. Because Archer's photographs were so rare, many collectors wanted them. Mr. Judd had the chance to buy a few of them for $60,000.

I almost fell out of my chair. Dad's hobby was taking pictures. Could it be that, a hundred years from now, Dad's photos would be worth that much?

"This is very exciting, Lester. I can hardly wait to set eyes upon these antiques," Dad said to Mr. Judd.

"They're all studies of young street waifs," said Mrs. Judd.

"What are waifs?" asked Nicky.

Mr. Judd explained. Back in the late 1800s in London, many poor children lived alone in the streets. They were called waifs. They had no parents and no one to care for them. They slept in alleys and empty buildings. For food, they either stole, begged, or starved. Sometimes, they earned a few pennies doing hard work.

© Houghton Mifflin Harcourt Publishing Company

Selection 14
Core Skills Reading Comprehension, Grade 5

Nicky and I couldn't believe that children could be treated so wickedly. When Mrs. Judd took out a folder of faded photos, we joined Dad in looking at them.

"Oh!" we exclaimed as we studied the pictures of ragged, mistreated children.

Two pictures of the same little girl interested me. She was beautiful, with huge, dark eyes. In one picture, I saw her back as she struggled with a heavy wheelbarrow. Her hair was a mop of dirty tangles hanging almost to her waist. Nicky was more interested in a photo of a skinny boy holding a torn coat around him. Both children looked starved and sad.

"I think the experts are right," said Dad. "The materials seem to be the correct ones for 1860. I've seen some of Archer's photos in a museum. They had the same sort of brownish coloring."

Mr. Judd said, "But none of the experts will state for certain that these are real Archer photographs and not forgeries. I would like to buy them, but I'm a little concerned."

Then the Judds started to talk about another expert from Washington, DC, who was going to arrive on Monday to test the old pictures.

"If they're not forgeries, I wish I had enough money to buy one," Dad said. "I would love to have it in my collection."

Nicky could not stop examining the photos of waifs. We weren't allowed to handle the pictures, but Mrs. Judd spread them out so that we could see them better. I only looked again to see what Nicky was staring at for so long.

Finally, Nicky spoke. "I don't know what it is, but there's something wrong with the wrinkles in the kids' clothes."

"Nicky, what can you know about 1860?" I said.

Then I suddenly realized that I wasn't doing what I always told everyone else to do. To be a detective, you must look and listen carefully and then think. I started to listen carefully to my brother.

"What do you mean?" I asked, bending over the pictures once more.

Nicky pointed to the beautiful little girl. "Look at those messy, ragged clothes. But in with all the wrinkles, under her hair, I can just make out two straight lines."

I could hardly tell what he was looking at. "Do you have a magnifying glass?" I asked Mrs. Judd.

She laughed, but she handed us one.

"It's on the boy, too," Nicky whispered to me. "It's strange."

We peered through the magnifying glass. I got excited. Nicky was right. I saw something else that seemed out of place. I said nothing aloud because I didn't want the Judds to laugh at us.

Nicky and I needed to check some of the odd things we had noticed in the pictures. We looked in the last volume of the Judds' encyclopedia. Some of what we were looking for wasn't in the encyclopedia. We were lucky, though. We found enough information by using the index in another book.

Nicky and I decided we would tell Dad what we had discovered. Then he could tell the Judds. We were afraid they would think we were silly. But our plan, as usual, didn't work exactly right.

Mrs. Judd inquired, "Are you ready to report your expert findings yet?" She looked at us. The expression on her face seemed to say, "Let's be patient with these kids playing detective."

I said, "Yes, but we may be wrong because it's hard to see much on those dirty, creased clothes. There is something unusual here. Nicky noticed that most of the wrinkles go in all directions, but there are also little lines that go only straight up and down. On the back of the little girl, almost hidden by her hair, we saw the same straight lines. With the magnifying glass, we figured out that there's a long zipper down the back of her dress. See it there." I pointed.

"Most of the shots of her show the front only, so it's hard to notice. Once we knew what to look for, we found that all the boy waifs have zippers on their clothes, too. Only tiny parts of them can be seen." I stopped.

Then Nicky said, "Zippers weren't invented until 1893. They were first used on clothes in 1931. Kids in 1860 could not have had zippers. The photos *have* to be forgeries. Donna noticed something, too. See the skinny little waif who looks as if he is starving?"

I reported on my find. "The hands holding the ragged coat around the waif's bony chest hardly show. With the magnifying glass, though, you can barely see the end of one of those sticky bandages you put on cuts. In one of Mr. Judd's books, we read that they weren't invented until the 1940s."

"Someone dishonest is playing a trick on old photo collectors!" exclaimed Dad.

What compliments were showered on us! Mr. and Mrs. Judd piled praise on Nicky and me until even our proud father turned red with embarrassment.

Mr. Judd said, "I could have lost a lot of money. Instead of paying an expert to fly in from Washington, I should have asked Donna and Nicky for help. I'm very grateful to you."

107

Name _____ Date _____

A Circle the correct answer for each question.

1. Based on the selection, in 1861

   a. photography was invented.

   b. photography was in its most popular period.

   c. the art of photography was in its early stages.

   d. photographers used the same materials as they do today.

2. Why was Mr. Judd worried about buying the photographs?

   a. The paper the photographs were printed on was not the kind used in 1860.

   b. He was not certain that the photographs had really been taken by Archer.

   c. He did not have enough money to buy the expensive photographs.

   d. The photographs were too faded to be Archer's work.

3. What did Donna and Nicky discover about the photographs?

   a. They were forgeries.   **c.** They were too faded.

   b. They were too wrinkled.   **d.** They were taken in the 1860s.

4. What important clue helped Donna and Nicky solve this case?

   a. seeing the wrong kind of zippers on the clothing

   b. seeing the clothing held together by sticky bandages

   c. seeing that the girl's hair was hanging almost to her waist

   d. seeing things that had not yet been invented in the 1860s

5. In this detective case, who was the better detective?

   a. Donna, because she did not care if the Judds thought her ideas were silly

   b. Nicky, because he did not care if the Judds thought his ideas were silly

   c. Donna, because she looked and listened carefully the entire time

   d. Nicky, because he looked and listened carefully the entire time

6. The two young detectives were not sure what the clues in the photographs meant. How did they check their information?

   a. by researching   **c.** by working at the library

   b. by asking experts   **d.** by making thoughtful guesses

7. Which phrase *best* expresses the theme of this selection?

   a. Silence Is Golden

   b. Do Well in Whatever You Do

   c. Buyer, Beware

   d. Great Things from Small Beginnings

Selection 14

Core Skills Reading Comprehension, Grade 5

Name _____ Date _____

B On each line are two words that are antonyms, or opposite in meaning. Circle the antonyms.

1. pouring   difficult   simple   flooded

2. creased   repaired   broke   exchanged

3. strange   ragged   embarrassed   familiar

4. behind   farther   upon   closer

5. supply   tumble   mumble   shout

6. huge   filthy   starved   spotless

7. examined   inquired   invented   replied

8. completed   struggled   started   commanded

C Choose a word to complete each sentence.

forgeries	peer	miserable	expert
mistreat	magnify	creases	antique

1. To make something larger to see it more clearly is to _____.

2. Someone who is very unhappy, upset, or ill is _____.

3. False copies that are claimed to be the real thing are _____.

4. To treat badly is to _____.

5. An _____ is someone who knows a lot about a subject.

6. An object used long ago is known as an _____.

7. Wrinkles are also called _____.

8. To examine something closely, you _____ at it.

D A time line is a good way to put events in the correct order. It can also be used to organize some kinds of materials into a shorter, more easily readable form. To fill out a time line, you must understand dates. Start with the earliest date at the left of the line and continue adding dates in order until the latest date is at the right end of the line. Place these dates in the correct places on the time line below. Then complete the time chart that follows by placing the events and their dates in correct order.

The History of Cameras

1720—The idea of using film to take pictures was first considered.

1568—A lens was placed on the hole in a box for a clearer view. The picture was reversed.

1830—Daguerre learned how to take a picture that lasted. It took an hour to make the photograph.

1850—Archer invented a better way to make negatives.

1822—Photographs were printed on a glass plate. It took eight hours to make the picture.

1569—A mirror was placed behind the lens in the box so pictures would not be reversed.

1841—Talbot invented the negative so that pictures could be copied over and over.

1553—A box with a hole in it was made to focus a picture for artists.

Time Line

_____

Time Chart

Date	Event
1553	A box with a hole in it was made to focus a picture for artists.
1568	

E When looking up information, you usually find many facts about a subject. Some are relevant for what you need. Some are not relevant. *Relevant* means *important for your purposes.*

Read the passage and facts below. Put an *X* by each fact that is not relevant to the passage.

Elizabeth Drake was the daughter of wealthy parents. In 1878, she read about the homeless waifs in a large English city. Elizabeth decided to start a soup kitchen, a place where children could be fed a free meal each day.

1. Elizabeth's grandmother gave her a large sum of money to buy meat, fish, and potatoes.

2. Many waifs could be found in the alleys around the harbor.

3. A merchant offered some land he owned near the harbor to use as a small park for the children of Elizabeth's friends and their nursemaids.

4. Elizabeth's parents gave her a trip to France for her eighteenth birthday.

5. Elizabeth's uncle let her live with him free of charge.

6. There was an empty store on a street facing the harbor that could be used as a soup kitchen.

7. Some of Elizabeth's cousins offered to spend one day a week helping at the soup kitchen.

8. Grocers gave free stale bread and leftover vegetables to use in the soup.

111

Name _____   Date _____

Skills Review: Selections 12–14

A The sentences in each group contain words with multiple meanings. Decide what the meaning of the underlined word is in the first sentence. Then write an *X* next to the sentence below it that contains a word with the same meaning as the word in the first sentence.

1. Sammy <u>plants</u> a tree with his grandmother whenever he goes to visit her.

   _____ **a.** Those chemical <u>plants</u> produce less pollution now than in years past.

   _____ **b.** The garden was filled with <u>plants</u> that Maura had never seen before.

   _____ **c.** Anyone who <u>plants</u> seeds has something to look forward to in a few days.

   _____ **d.** When Palak gets angry, he <u>plants</u> his feet on the ground and refuses to move.

2. What <u>part</u> of the lesson do you not understand?

   _____ **a.** Rosa still doesn't know what her <u>part</u> will be in the play.

   _____ **b.** Benjamin's father did not want to <u>part</u> from his family, but he had no choice.

   _____ **c.** Mom left one <u>part</u> of the job for you do to.

   _____ **d.** <u>Part</u> your hair on the other side for a change.

3. The man's <u>face</u> was familiar.

   _____ **a.** The new houses in the neighborhood <u>face</u> the park.

   _____ **b.** If you don't <u>face</u> your problems, you'll never solve them.

   _____ **c.** The <u>face</u> of the cliff was dotted with pelicans' nests.

   _____ **d.** Kelly has a round <u>face</u>.

4. Mr. Torres, <u>step</u> carefully because the sidewalk is icy.

   _____ **a.** The top <u>step</u> has a hole in it.   _____ **c.** The second <u>step</u> is to peel the fruit.

   _____ **b.** If you see an anthill, <u>step</u> around it.   _____ **d.** The baby took her first <u>step</u> today!

B On the line before each word, write the letter of every meaning that fits.

_____ **1.** jam   **a.** the sound a dog makes   **f.** a twig

_____ **2.** bark   **b.** to become fixed in place with   **g.** to pierce with something sharp
                                glue
_____ **3.** stick   **h.** to make a part of your body
                            c. a curved part of a road   not straight
_____ **4.** bend   **d.** to fill something up completely   **i.** something made with fruit to
                                                                      eat on bread
                            e. the outside part of a tree

Name _____ Date _____

 Read the selection about two U.S. presidents. Then complete the Venn diagram by circling the letter of the information that correctly goes in each part of it.

Two Roosevelts

Two men served the United States as "President Roosevelt." Theodore was the first President Roosevelt. His family had a great deal of money, and he was active in politics. He became a member of the Republican Party. In 1884, Theodore suffered a terrible tragedy when his wife and mother died on the same day. He recovered and went on to serve as governor of New York. Then he served as vice president for President McKinley in 1900. When McKinley died in 1901, Theodore Roosevelt became president. He started the national parks system, and he helped build the Panama Canal. In his last run for president, Theodore Roosevelt lost to William Howard Taft.

Franklin D. Roosevelt was the second President Roosevelt. His family also had a great deal of money, but Franklin was a Democrat. Franklin's life was not always easy. He got polio as a young man. The illness made it hard for him to walk. Franklin went on to become governor of New York, too. He was then elected president in 1932. Like Theodore, Franklin did many great things. He started job programs when many people were out of work. He led the country during World War II. He was elected president each time he ran. He died in 1945 during his fourth term.

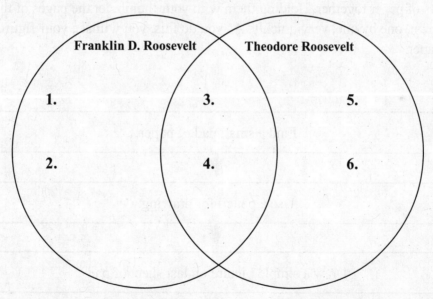

Franklin D. Roosevelt   **Theodore Roosevelt**

1.   3.   5.

2.   4.   6.

1. a. Was lieutenant governor of New York
    b. Was a Democrat

2. a. Came from a poor family
    b. Died while he was president

3. a. Served as vice president
    b. Came from a wealthy family

4. a. Suffered a tragedy as an adult
    b. Became president when the previous president died

5. a. Started the national parks system
    b. Started job programs

6. a. Was a Republican
    b. Led the country during World War II

113

D Read the following how-to selection. Then use information to complete the flow chart, which shows the first steps for making a flip book.

Making Flip Books

Flip books are a fun and easy way to make cartoon movies. To make a flip book, you need a pad of paper, a pen or pencil, and your imagination.

First, find a small pad of paper, or use the bottom corner of a notebook. You will also need a dark pen or pencil to draw the pictures in your flip book. It might be better to use a pencil in case you need to erase mistakes or you decide to change your ideas. Later, you can draw over your pencil marks with a pen.

Next, turn to the last sheet of the pad and draw a simple picture. You might draw a small flower blowing in a breeze or a small dog barking.

Using the image from the bottom sheet, trace an image that is almost the same, with some slight changes on the second sheet. If you are drawing a dog barking, for example, draw a dog with his mouth closed in this picture. Once you have finished the second sheet, turn over the third sheet and continue drawing, changing the picture just a little bit each time.

When you finish drawing on all the sheets, put the pad on a table and pull up all the sheets of paper together. Holding them with your thumb, let the pages of the pad "flip" down, one by one, very quickly. As you do this, you will see your figure "move" on the paper.

Find a small pad of paper.
↓
Use a pencil for drawing.
↓
Draw a simple picture on last sheet of pad.
↓

Name _____ Date _____

 Study this portion of a glossary from a book for children titled *Let's Learn About the Circulatory System.* **Then answer the questions.**

Glossary

artery • a blood vessel that carries blood away from the heart (p. 14)

capillary • a tiny blood vessel with very thin walls; oxygen, nutrients, and waste material pass through the walls (p. 16)

nutrient • a material that food supplies to the body; the body uses nutrients for growing, getting energy, and repairing itself (p. 7)

plasma • the liquid part of blood; it carries nutrients, blood cells, and waste materials (p. 6)

platelet • a cell without a nucleus that is found in the blood; platelets help the bleeding stop when you cut yourself

red blood cell • a cell that carries oxygen from the lungs to other places in the body (p. 8)

vein • a blood vessel that carries blood back to the heart (p. 15)

white blood cell • a cell that helps to protect your body by fighting germs (p. 9)

---

1. After what entry in the glossary would an entry for *circulatory system* appear?

   _____

2. On which page does the word *vein* first appear in the book?

   _____

3. Which words in the definition of *plasma* are defined in the glossary?

   _____

4. Which word in the entry for *artery* would readers probably like to see in the glossary as a separate entry?

   _____

5. Which three things defined in the glossary are all vessels?

   _____

6. Does the word *pulse* appear in the book?

   _____

F Circle two antonyms in each group of words below.

1. experiment   contract   dissolve   expand

2. tension   inquired   replied   forgery

3. miserable   uncooperative   happy   familiar

4. liquid   condensation   embarrassed   unashamed

5. decrease   crease   cease   increase

6. unafraid   frightened   rare   solid

7. negative   positive   evaporate   complain

8. filthy   clean   hobby   photograph

9. sturdy   moist   continue   dry

10. rare   expert   trusted   undependable

11. decrease   rough   important   gentle

G Place the dates below on the time line in correct order. Then read the dates and information in order so that you will have a better idea about the history of the United States.

1836—The battle of the Alamo took place in Texas.

1492—Columbus came to the Americas.

1918—World War I ended.

1607—Jamestown was founded.

1969—People landed on the moon.

1776—The Declaration of Independence was signed.

1941—Pearl Harbor was attacked.

Answer Key

Selection 1: pages 1–4

A 1. b   3. c
    2. a   4. d

B 1. to explain why people such as the Montgolfier brothers worked hard to find a way to travel through the air
    2. They wanted to see how safe flying was before they made humans risk their lives.

C 1. command   6. soar
    2. jealous   7. plunged
    3. vehicle   8. myth
    4. constructed   9. imitate
    5. spectacular   10. plummet

D Sentence order: 3, 6, 5, 1, 2, 4

Selection 2: pages 5–8

A 1. b   2. a

B 1. d   3. c
    2. b

C 1. Sample answer: In both experiments, heated air made something rise. Yet in the experiment described in "Up, Up, and Away," a balloon rose, and heated air from burning paper made it rise. In the experiment described in "Two Brothers Who Envied Birds," a bag rose, and hot smoke inside it made it rise.
    2. Sample answer: Answers will vary but should include the following: The brothers lived in a time in which people believed they could do anything with the aid of science. The brothers were excellent observers. They conducted many experiments before being successful with their invention.
    3. Sample answer: It is easier to tell how the author feels about the Montgolfier brothers in "Up, Up, and Away." The author says that they were excellent observers and praises them by saying that they were pioneers and had succeeded in "proving that human flight could be a reality." In "Two Brothers Who Envied Birds," the author simply gives facts about the brothers and does not express any opinions about them or their achievements.

D Circle:
    1. a, c, d   2. a, c, e

E 1. e   4. d
    2. b   5. a
    3. f

Selection 3: pages 9–16

A 1. b   5. c
    2. d   6. c
    3. b   7. d
    4. a   8. c

B 1. Sample answer: Ellen reacted as you would expect. She was very frightened, and she turned pale and shrieked, "What is happening?" The narrator didn't have a big reaction. Instead, she felt as if she was only observing the strange events around her.
    2. Sample answer: In this paragraph, the narrator was finally affected by having survived an earthquake, and the fear she hadn't felt before finally came out. Also, what happened to her in this paragraph is what caused the word *earthquake* to have true meaning for her later.
    3. Sample answer: By doing this, the reader could find out about the events in the story and also know what Lucy was feeling as those events happened. In addition, the reader could find out how Lucy felt about really knowing the meaning of the word *earthquake*.

C 1. tourists   8. shrieked
    2. vibrate   9. violently
    3. survived   10. devastation
    4. illuminate   11. canceled
    5. anticipation   12. underdog
    6. stadium   13. elation
    7. spectators   14. throng

D 1. Engineers have learned from earlier earthquakes.
    2. Engineers now know . . . different kinds of subsoil.
    3. The newer ways . . . resist earthquake damage.
    4. Today, all parts . . . support one another.

E 1. Underline: Large plates grinding . . . cause earthquakes.
    Write: If they meet and bump, they cause tremors in the earth.
    2. Underline: Just as in earthquakes, . . . bump into each other and separate.
    Write: Then all the melted rock, flame, gas, ashes, and stones erupt into the air.
    3. Underline: Earthquakes occurring anywhere set off huge waves under the ocean.
    Write: These waves, called **tsunamis**, are over 100 feet high and travel 500 miles an hour.
    4. Underline: There are steps you can take to protect yourself during an earthquake.
    Write: Find a solid, strong piece of furniture such as a desk or a table and crawl under it, so falling glass and plaster will not hit you.

F 1. Tigers, lions, leopards, . . . before a volcano erupted. Before a forest fire, . . . from the woods.

117

2. Hurricanes are identified . . .
   assigned to them.
   Some dishes . . . even in
   earthquakes.
   The surface of the earth . . .
   calm and comfortable.
3. Tornadoes can also destroy
   buildings.
   The lava from a volcano can
   cause a great deal of damage.

Selection 4: pages 17–24

A 1. a   4. d
   2. a   5. a
   3. b   6. c

B 1. c
   2. two
   3. quarrel; question
   4. a loose, deep, wet sand
      deposit in which a heavy
      object or person may sink
   5. quill
   6. place from which to get stone
   7. three
   8. quarry
   9. fast; speedy; rapid; swift
  10. queen

C 1. 27–29; 52–55
   2. 68–79
   3. 31–43
   4. 11
   5. b
   6. because additional
      information is found under
      the subtopic rivers

D 1. 12
   2. 2; 9
   3. 8; 9
   4. A–Bo; Ho–Kn; Ne–Po

E 1. F   5. N
   2. T   6. F
   3. T   7. T
   4. N   8. F

F 1. a   4. c
   2. b   5. b
   3. a   6. b

Selection 5: pages 25–36

A 1. d   6. c
   2. b   7. a
   3. d   8. d
   4. c   9. c
   5. b

B 1. Sample answer: The story
      says that when the twins
      were hiding in the hut, they
      "giggled" and "smiled" until
      they realized "their prank had
      been discovered."
   2. Sample answer: by showing
      what the hoofprints made by
      the iron horseshoes looked
      like; by showing what a lord
      and lady in 1280 might look
      like

C 1. suggestion   4. suggest
   2. suggested   5. suggesting
   3. suggesting

D 1. e   6. i
   2. c   7. g
   3. a   8. k
   4. f   9. d
   5. j   10. b

E 1. tower   6. door
   2. wall   7. portcullis
   3. moat   8. banner
   4. courtyard   9. battlements
   5. drawbridge   10. Great Hall

F 1. light; i   5. light; g
   2. forge; d   6. light; k
   3. forge; c   7. tower; b
   4. light; j   8. forge; f

G 1. connection   5. inspection
   2. actions   6. construction
   3. location   7. direction
   4. invitations   8. directions

H 1. a   5. b
   2. c   6. b
   3. c   7. a
   4. a   8. b

Selection 6: pages 37–41

A 1. b   4. a
   2. d   5. c
   3. a   6. c

B Sample answer: Walter thought
it was a funny trick that would
amuse him and make him feel
less bored. The villagers thought
it was a mean thing to do
because it interrupted their work.

C 1. someone who is not a
      character; someone who is
      not a character

2. make people believe there is a
     unicorn; make people believe
     there is a wolf
3. no one will trust you if you
     play tricks; no one will trust
     you if you play tricks
4. happy; sad
5. Paragraphs will vary but
     should include the following:
     In both stories, the narrator
     is not a character in the story.
     Enid and Edward fool Lady
     Isabel and Lord John into
     thinking there is a unicorn;
     Walter tricks the villagers into
     thinking a wolf is about to
     attack his sheep. The lesson
     that Enid and Edward and
     Walter learn is the same: No
     one will trust you if you play
     tricks on people. The ending
     of "To Gain Something Lost"
     is happy, but the ending of
     "The Boy Who Cried Wolf" is
     sad.

D 1. mistrust   6. reorder
   2. impatient   7. misunderstand
   3. restate   8. unexpected
   4. imperfect   9. misbehave
   5. unusual

E 1. resend   4. reset
   2. unable   5. unprotected
   3. impolite

Skills Review: Selections 1–6 pages 42–47

A 1. direction   8. occurrence
   2. directing   9. occurs
   3. directed   10. occurrence
   4. directly   11. occurred
   5. direct   12. occurred
   6. direction   13. occurring
   7. occur

B Across
   1. dismount   15. fled
   5. inspect   17. we
   7. go   18. amaze
   9. capture   19. bridge
  10. on   20. scene
  11. excite   21. shepherd
  13. net

Down

1. dragon   8. one
2. moat   9. cellars
3. unicorn   12. ill
4. forge   14. towers
6. steward   16. dashed

C 1. A saddle is a seat used by a person riding on a horse.
   2. That's why I'm two hours late for school, Mr. Patel.
   3. Autumn was bringing its many changes.
   4. Sometimes, sailors landed on islands in the Pacific Ocean to get fresh water and food.

D Matilda and Thomas were very busy before school. *Or,* Matilda and Thomas did a lot of work before going to school.

E 1. dictionary
   2. index
   3. table of contents
   4. encyclopedia
   5. table of contents
   6. index; table of contents
   7. dictionary
   8. map

F 1. 28–30   5. 2
   2. 6   6. no
   3. no   7. 142
   4. 35   8. no
   9. cymbals, drums, guitar, piano
   10. between *Chinese* and *Indian*

G 1. c   3. c
   2. a   4. b

H 1. b   4. d
   2. c   5. f
   3. a

Selection 7: pages 48–56

A 1. a   5. c
   2. c   6. c
   3. d   7. b
   4. d

B 1. Sample answer: He was making fun of Joanne's last name—Smart. His joke was that anyone who was "Smart" must have a brain that was larger than usual.

2. Sample answer: Donna Chang uses her detective skills to figure out information about a new girl at school. The girl's last name is Smart. After Donna tells other students about the girl, they like and respect her so much that they never tease her about her name.

3. Sample answer: The art shows that Joanne is not completely happy to be at a new school. Instead, her look shows that she is expecting someone to make fun of her last name.

C Sample answer: watch carefully: studies Joanne's appearance as she is standing next to the school door listen carefully: hears Mrs. Jordan tell Liz about the new girl; listens to Liz say the new girl's last name think: thinks about Joanne's expression, the bump on a finger, her tennis shoes, and her jacket

D 1. j   8. c
   2. l   9. n *or* g
   3. f   10. b
   4. a   11. g
   5. m   12. o
   6. h   13. d
   7. k   14. i

E Answers will vary.

F 1. D   5. M.I.
   2. X   6. X
   3. D   7. D
   4. D   8. D

Selection 8: pages 57–67

A The police should have closed the street, but they did not. It probably prevented even more accidents.

B *Kakapos:* 12
check ✔ (for facts): 1, 2, 4, 5, 6, 7, 10, 11, 12, 13, 14, 15
mark X (for opinions): 3, 8, 9

Guacharos: 11
check ✔: 1, 2, 4, 5, 8, 10, 11, 12, 13, 14, 15; mark X: 3, 6, 7, 9

Quack Grass: 12
check ✔: 1, 3, 4, 5, 6, 7, 8, 10, 12, 13, 14, 15; mark X: 2, 9, 11

C 1. steep   9. prevent
   2. errors   10. disappoint
   3. remark   11. immediately
   4. opinions   12. rely
   5. approach   13. attractive
   6. compliment   14. accident
   7. sprout   15. article
   8. rhizomes

Selection 9: pages 68–73

A 1. c   6. b
   2. d   7. b
   3. c   8. d
   4. d   9. d
   5. d

B 1. 4
   2. corn syrup, chicle, sugar, flavoring
   3. sugar
   4. flavoring
   5. corn syrup, chicle
   6. chicle
   7. chicle
   8. the ingredients in modern chewing gum

C 1. cherry
   2. grape
   3. banana and strawberry
   4. about 4,900
   5. about 5,900
   6. mixed fruit
   7. grape
   8. favorite gum flavors among school children

D 1. 8,000
   2. Canada
   3. Germany
   4. 7,500
   5. 2,500
   6. United States and England; France and Russia
   7. 5,000
   8. how much sugarless gum was chewed in the world in 1980

Selection 10: pages 74–81

A   The Linnaea
   I. What the Linnaea looks like
   II. Where the Linnaea grows
   III. How to grow Linnaeas

119

B   The Tulip Poplar
   A. Tallest broadleaf tree
   B. Two hundred feet high
   C. Wide trunk
   D. Beautiful, yellow,
      tulip-like blossoms
   E. Notched leaves
   F. White bark
   G. Yellow inner wood

   A. Eastern U.S.
   B. As far west as Arkansas
     1. Tennessee
     2. Kentucky
     3. Indiana

   A. Furniture
   B. Baskets
   C. Boxes
   D. Ornaments

C   The Tailorbird
  I. Has unusual nesting habits
   A. Puts two broad leaves
      together
     1. Stabs holes in edges
     2. Uses web to sew leaves
       together
   B. Nest looks like a sack with
      open top
   C. Lines the nest
     1. Uses silky threads from
       plants
     2. Uses soft grass
     3. Uses animals' hairs
   D. Hides nest in thick bushes
   E. Lays two or three speckled
      eggs
  II. Has unusual appearance
   A. Is four to six inches long
   B. Has thin, sharp bill
   C. Has red head
   D. Has olive green back and
      light gray front
   E. Has long tail that sticks up
      straight
 III. Found in few places
   A. Lives only in cleared areas
   B. Lives in gardens and on
      farms
   C. Lives in India, East Indies,
      and the Philippine Islands

D
1. Title
2. Subtopics
3. Main idea
4. Additional
   details for
   subtopics
5. Subtopics
6. Subtopics
7. Main idea
8. Subtopics

E
1. b
2. d
3. c
4. c
5. a
6. d
7. c
8. a

F
1. appearance
2. speckled
3. comfortable
4. graceful
5. pleasant
6. expensive
7. pouch
8. reeds
9. blossoms
10. evergreen
11. outstanding
12. notched

Selection 11: pages 82–86

A   Puffins
   A. Arctic waters of Atlantic
      and Pacific Oceans
   B. Iceland
   C. Great Britain
   D. Maine
  II. What puffins look like
   A. Odd-looking
   B. Top part of body is black
   C. Underside and cheeks are
      white
   D. Adults are the size of a
      young duck
   E. Large, red feet
   F. Unusually large head
     1. Beak like a parrot
     2. Beak covered with
       heavy plates
     3. Plates are round and red,
       yellow, and blue.
     4. Plates lost after mating
 III. Their useful beaks
   A. Used in fighting
   B. Used to attract mates
   C. Used as shovel during
      nesting
   D. Used to carry food
 IV. Expert at fishing
   A. Catches different kinds of
      sea animals
   B. Beak can hold up to ten
      fish

B
1. gulls
2. 1920–1923; 1934–1937
3. 1940
4. 1960
5. 1925–1930
6. 6,000
7. 5,000
8. about 6,200
9. There were one thousand
   fewer puffins than gulls.

C
1. 40	7. Canada
2. 160	8. 980
3. 20	9. Europe
4. 220	10. 840
5. India	11. 140
6. 1,120	12. 280

D
1. char
2. herring
3. smelt
4. herring and cod
5. 50
6. char
7. cod
8. smelt
9. shrimp and char
10. in zoos in Great Britain

Skills Review: Selections 7–11 pages 87–92

A
1. d
2. b
3. Uses dorsal fin to jab enemies
4. Answers will vary.
5. The person may become
   unconscious, paralyzed, or be
   killed.
6. It hides in the sand and moves
   away slowly.
7. Crown of thorns starfish
   attacks only to defend itself.
8. starfish
9. spines
10. stingers
11. dorsal fin
12. tail
13. how the stingray uses barbed
   stingers for defense
14. Stonefish venom may cause
   paralysis or death.

120

B Across
1. masticate   12. squirm
6. cap   14. tune
8. rely   15. fizz
9. popular   16. dependable

Down
2. adult   8. relief
3. chicle   10. resin
4. trophy   11. amazed
5. disappointed 13. quit
7. sprout

C   Animal Disguises
   A. Protect from enemies
   B. Warn enemies of horrible taste or sting
   C. Help increase the species

   A. Body shape like a twig
   B. Green wings like leaves
   C. Two or three inches long
   D. Green or brown

III. Fish that looks like a dead leaf
   B. When caught, lies flat like a leaf
   C. When caught, is usually tossed back

IV. Toad that looks like a leaf
   A. Sharp snout like pointed end of leaf
   C. Two small black spots like holes in a leaf

D 1. spines
   2. tails and fangs
   3. fins
   4. 100%
   5. 13%
   6. They store venom in spines.
   7. 20%
   8. where venom is stored in sea animals

Selection 12: pages 93–97

A 1. b   5. b
   2. c   6. a
   3. c   7. c
   4. d

B 1. Sample answer: Rachel does not want to play the piano anymore because she thinks she will never be as good as her father. At first, she does not want to tell her father this, and she makes up the reason that the music is boring.
   2. Sample answer: Rachel compares the songs she is playing to dirt because for most people dirt is not very interesting.
   3. Sample answer: At the beginning, the sounds are of many starts and stops and of wrong notes being played, followed by keys being banged. At the end, the sounds are of a cheerful song being played. This shows that Rachel has changed the way she thinks about playing the piano and that she will enjoy it more in the future.
   4. Sample answer: At the beginning, Rachel does not want to play the piano anymore because she thinks she will never play well enough. At the end, she is enjoying playing the piano so much that she does want to stop practicing.

C Sample answer: *Same:* plays the piano. *Dad:* gives concerts; does not make a lot of mistakes; wants to keep playing the piano. *Rachel:* does not give concerts; makes a lot of mistakes; does not want to keep playing the piano

D 1. 5
   2. a written symbol used in music
   3. d

Selection 13: pages 98–104

A 1. d   4. a
   2. c   5. c
   3. a   6. c

B first box: Cut a strip of paper for the scale.
last box: Set the funnel inside the container.
C 1. insulator
   2. 4
   3. 13
   4. electron; proton
   5. It is possible that *shock* appears in the book but was not included in the glossary.
   6. Place "charge" before "closed circuit."
D 1. b   3. a
   2. d
E 1. sounds heard during a rainstorm
   2. Sample answer: The speaker is very happy because of the rainstorm. She says that she is a "joyous spectator" and applauds because she is enjoying "nature's majestic performance." She dances playfully through puddles. She thinks the raindrops taste "sweet."

F Taste: sweet drops of rain. Sight: stanzas 1, 3; sun vanishes, clouds advance; brilliant colors weave together; clouds unlock, water cascades down, shower cleans the ground. Hearing: stanza 2; thunder bellows, leaves rustle, wind whistles, sound of raindrops

Selection 14: pages 105–112

A 1. c   5. d
   2. b   6. a
   3. a   7. c
   4. d

B 1. difficult; simple
   2. repaired; broke
   3. strange, familiar
   4. farther; closer
   5. mumble; shout
   6. filthy; spotless
   7. inquired; replied
   8. completed; started

121

C
1. magnify
2. miserable
3. forgeries
4. mistreat
5. expert
6. antique
7. creases
8. peer

D 1553, 1568, 1569, 1720, 1822, 1830, 1841, 1850

1568 A lens was placed on the hole in the box for a clearer view. The picture was reversed.

1569 A mirror was placed behind the lens in the box so pictures would not be reversed.

1720 The idea of using film to take pictures was first considered.

1822 Photographs were printed on a glass plate. It took eight hours to make the picture.

1830 Daguerre learned how to take a picture that lasted. It took an hour to make the photograph.

1841 Talbot invented the negative so that pictures could be copied over and over.

1850 Archer invented a better way to make negatives.

E 3, 4, 5

Skills Review: Selections 12–14 pages 112–116

A
1. c
2. c
3. d
4. b

B
1. d; i
2. a; e
3. b; f; g
4. c; h

C
1. b
2. b
3. b
4. a
5. a
6. a

D Trace the image from the first sheet and make a slight change on the second sheet.

E
1. capillary
2. 15
3. nutrients; blood cells
4. vessel
5. artery; capillary; vein
6. It is possible that *pulse* is used but was not included in the glossary.

F
1. contract, expand
2. inquired, replied
3. miserable, happy
4. embarrassed, unashamed
5. decrease, increase
6. unafraid, frightened
7. negative, positive
8. filthy, clean
9. moist, dry
10. trusted, undependable
11. rough, gentle

G 1492, 1607, 1776, 1836, 1918, 1941, 1969